$ENTREPRENEUR COMMUNICATION$
TO COMMUNICATE IS TO SUCCEED

We Don't Listen to Understand,
We Listen to Reply

Daniel R. Hogan Jr., Ph.D. MBA

authorHOUSE®

AuthorHouse™
1663 Liberty Drive
Bloomington, IN 47403
www.authorhouse.com
Phone: 1 (800) 839-8640

© 2018 Daniel R. Hogan Jr., Ph.D. MBA All rights reserved.

No part of this book may be reproduced, stored in a retrieval system, or transmitted by any means without the written permission of the author.

Published by AuthorHouse 07/24/2018

ISBN: 978-1-5462-4971-9 (sc)
ISBN: 978-1-5462-4970-2 (e)

Library of Congress Control Number: 2018908581

Print information available on the last page.

Any people depicted in stock imagery provided by Getty Images are models, and such images are being used for illustrative purposes only.
Certain stock imagery © Getty Images.

This book is printed on acid-free paper.

Because of the dynamic nature of the Internet, any web addresses or links contained in this book may have changed since publication and may no longer be valid. The views expressed in this work are solely those of the author and do not necessarily reflect the views of the publisher, and the publisher hereby disclaims any responsibility for them.

DEDICATION

A Concise, Succinct Thank-You to my Loved Ones.

TABLE OF CONTENTS

Preface ix
Introduction xiii
Chapter 1   Goals and Foundations 1
Chapter 2   Meetings And Teams 7
Chapter 3   The Business Plan 21
Chapter 4   Effective Public Speaking 43
Chapter 5   Effective Written Communication 49
Chapter 6   Resumes 57
Chapter 7   Grammar Revisted 67
Chapter 8   Intercultural Communication 73
Chapter 9   Ethics 77
Chapter 10   Marketing 111
Final Thoughts 119
About The Author 121

APPENDIX

Appendix 1   Business Plan Outline 125
Appendix 1A   The Business Plan Presentation 139
Appendix 2   77 Questions Every Business Plan Should Answer ... 141
Appendix 3   Mission Statements 147
Appendix 4   Visual Aid Usage 149
Appendix 5   Ten Things That Will Get You Fired 151

Appendix 6	The Problem With Rules	153
Appendix 7	Communication Interview	155
Appendix 8	The Entrepreneurial Process to Start, Grow, and Manage A Business	157
Glossary		159

PREFACE

*"It ain't what you don't know that gets you into trouble.
It's what you know for sure that just ain't so."*
Mark Twain

Persistence, determination, attitude, and the ability to communicate are the keys to success.

All communication be it business, government, personal is between people. The ability to convey thoughts, ideas, information, and motivation is key to achieving progress and success. Managers of organizations have the basic job of gathering and distributing information, motivating and inspiring team effort toward a goal, and to make decisions. Internal communication takes place within people in an organization, owners, managers, supervisors, and employees. External communication takes place between the company and outside people, customers, vendors, and creditors. Effective communication is essential to accomplishing these goals.

There are ten basic commandments to establish this connection for successful human relations in all communication efforts.

1. Speak to people. There is nothing as nice as a cheerful word of greeting.

2. Smile at people. It takes 72 muscles to frown, only 14 to smile.

3. Call people by name. The sweetest music to anyone's ear is the sound of his/her own name.

4. Be friendly and helpful. If you would have friends, be friendly.

5. Be cordial. Speak and act as if everything you do is a genuine pleasure.

6. Be genuinely interested in people. You can learn to like everybody if you try.

7. Be generous with praise – cautious with criticism.
8. Be considerate with the feelings of others. It will be appreciated.
9. Be thoughtful of the opinions of others. There are three sides to a controversy – yours, the other fellow's, and the right one.
10. Be alert to fine service. What counts most in life is what we do for others.

ORGANIZATION

Business leaders and scholars from various disciplines have attempted to define the term "organization". A formal organization is defined by Louis (Allen Louis *Management and Organization,* McGraw-Hill) "the process of identifying and delegating responsibility and authority and establishing relationships for the purpose of enabling people to work most effectively in accomplishing objectives." And Barnard (Chester Barnard *The Function of the Executive,* Harvard Press) defines a formal organization as a "system of consciously coordinated activities of two or more people."

Accordingly, the three essential elements of an organization are:

- Common Purpose
- Willingness to serve and
- **Communication**

Most of the definitions of organizations appear to stress the following factors all requiring effective communication:

- Organization symbolizes a group effort
- The group effort is directed toward a goal
- The group effort can be achieved by coordination
- Authority and responsibility help to achieve coordination

Most of the firms of the early 1900s were small retailing and manufacturing enterprisers operating in a vacuum with little knowledge of social economic changes. Management was essentially informal, mainly because products or services were unsophisticated, as were the firm's production process and operations. Also contributing was the lack of intervening levels of management between the top manager (the owner) and workers. Insofar as subordinates were concerned, the supervisor or foreman was the ultimate authority, whose power was absolute. It was their task to instill a team effort through communication of goals, information, and procedures.

Most entrepreneurs (owners) possess an inner locus-of-control which hinders the very growth and development of their firms and often prevented them from creating a joint effort via effective communication to others. The very traits which sparked the enterprises often prove to be a serious problem. This need for control and distrust of delegation impacts the interrelationships which are vital to the success and growth of the business.

Entrepreneurs obsessed with being in control for fear of others controlling them, taking advantage, or making costly mistakes have little patience with employees who act with initiative and think for themselves. This micromanagement may have serve well as a start-up business, but now will stifle the development and restrict attracting the very assistance from others, be they employees, advisers, or vendors, required to grow a profitable business.

It is overcoming this difficulty that enables a business to mature and become a thriving, growing, profitable business rather than remain a lifestyle, small business, or a failed business. The expression that leaders and entrepreneurs do the right thing while managers simply do things right is not enough. Entrepreneurs who by necessity are also managers-owners must do it the right way to start, grow, and manage a profitable business that continues to build value. The transition of the visionary start-up entrepreneur to a pragmatic thinking leader aware of the economic climate and behaving in an ethical manner to all concern as an entrepreneur-manager willing to invest in learning the necessary management skills without fear of delegation to others while mastering the ability to communicate that vision in a motivating and inspirational manner is the mission of this book.

It was Will Rogers who commented that *"Common sense ain't necessarily common practice."* It is relatively easy to enumerate the best management practice, but another altogether to implement them.

Communication skills, both written and oral, are a learned skill achievable by all. They are the keys to success and all business leaders possess them.

All our communication, oral and written, skills and power come from learned behaviors and awareness observations of others. Whether it is to inspire, motivate, or acquiring cooperation and involvement; in an investment, credit application, or sales presentation to communicate in a clear understandable manner with greatly contribute to success.

Effective communication is positive and assertive. It influences the audience in as mutually beneficial way that creates the "you win, I win" scenario. This ability will share the vision and inspire others to work with you rather than for you.

> "TO UNDERSTAND IS HARD. ONCE ONE UNDERSTANDS, ACTION IS EASY."
> SUN YAT-SEN

INTRODUCTION

*"He was a self-made man who owed
his lack of success to nobody."*
Joseph Heller

The key to a healthy work relationship within an organization is based on managing its communications. It has been concluded that management's number one problem is a lack of effective communications. Communication is a two-way process. An employee cannot work with all his competence, ability, intelligence, and enthusiasm if the real purpose of the job is not known to him. Equally important is the opportunity for the employee to communicate and contribute to ideas and opinion relating to job performance before the manager makes the decision to assign it.

Communication is the process of trusting employees and advising them about the job, the business, and the future plans for them, the vision and mission of the organization. Effective communication requires a competent sender and an understanding receiver. <u>There is no communication if the receiver does not understand the message.</u>

Feedback, both positive and negative, completes the communication cycle.

Committees, conferences, meetings, group discussions, and distribution of written memorandums are methods by which good horizontal communication can be fostered.

Communications among teams are also effective and are usually centralized or decentralized. Centralized team members all consult and communicate through one individual to solve problems or perform task. In decentralized teams, all communicate with each other and upon reaching consensus move to the project at hand. The centralized approach is generally much faster and more efficient.

There are several barriers to good communication within an organization which must be identified to overcome them.

- Distance: The physical difference between management and the employees decreases the chance of face-to-face communication. This lack of face-to-face interchange leads towards misunderstandings of the project, job, mission, and vision of goals and objectives to be accomplished. Distance will also make it difficult to clarify and correct these misunderstandings.
- Differences: A major barrier to effective communication is the tendency to make value judgments on the statement of others. Managers and employees tend to interpret information and message considering their own views, values, opinions, and backgrounds rather than objectively.
- Semantics: The structure of the language and words used can lead to misrepresentations of the true meaning and nature of the intended communication. Words with multiple meanings or confusing context can lead to misinterpretation of the intended message.
- Lack of Trust: Based on experience, if a subordinate is reluctant to report bad news due to the possible unfavorable reflection on him, then such information will be withheld.
- Inaccessibility: If management is not available, too busy, for discussion or consultation then a communication breakdown will result. Subordinate motivation will be affected and rather than seeking management direction will relied on a trial and error approach to situations.
- Lack of Clear Responsibilities: Lack of duties, responsibilities, and authority results in status and role ambiguities.
- Personal Incompatibility: A communication block can result if managers and subordinate's personalities clash.
- Refusal to Listen: Due to careless attitudes or arrogant nature refusal to listen by both or either managers or subordinates will block effective communication.
- Failure to use Proper Media for message delivery: Several type of communication delivery systems are available within an organization, written memorandums, e-mails, and formal letters, verbal face-to-face, meetings, and group discussions,

electronic, fax, phone, group e-mail; the effectiveness will depend on choosing the proper media for the situation.
- Communication Gap: The formal communication networks are built along the authority-responsibility lines of the organization. As the organization grows, the network tends to become larger and more complex with little planning resulting in gaps in the communication delivery system. An over-reliance only on indirect formal communication methods rather than using other methods when the situation warrants with create defects.
- Over-Loading: When people are overloaded with information, they tend to perform poorly even lower than those with insufficient information.

Effective business communication within an organization faces many pitfalls. Most often the problem lies with the sender's failure to pinpoint the purpose of the message and with the lack of knowing how the receivers will perceive and understand the information and even if they are willing listeners. To avoid such pitfalls the communicator can do the following:

- Define the problem in understandable simple language for the listeners in terms of circumstances that have led to the purpose and urgency of the message to inform, persuade, and stimulate thought into action.
- Formulate and tailor the basic message by assembling relevant information to the interest of the recipients, developing the concept, and determining which is the best medium to use and often it would be wise to use several channels of communication.
- Get feedback and measure the results to determine if the message was truly understood. Remember that effective communication is a two-way process between senders and receivers with appropriate feedback to assure complete understanding.
- To build trust through communication often converse with everyone informally, evaluating the workplace culture and motivation, and learning employee's opinions and suggestion about recent organizational actions and decisions.

To be effective in any business environment or individually, the communicator, the sender of the message, must know the audience receiving the message and communicate in the language or manner that is readily understood. The message, the information, is only received and accepted when it is understood and invokes desired actions or new thoughts. Effective communication will manifest itself in several benefits for the organization:

- Increased productivity
- Improved and consistent work flow
- Stronger business, culture, and employee feedback
- Better decision making
- Better problem solving
- Improved professional image and employee/employer rapport

Good communication is a dynamic process consisting of six stages:

1. The sender has an idea to be communicated and wants to share it.

2. The sender decides on the best method to encode the idea to be effectively communicated. Depending on the audience, this consists of the actual words, method (oral or written), format (formal or informal), gestures, visual-aids, tone, and location.

3. The sender communicates the message. To transmit the information the sender must decide on the proper channel such as face-to-face, telephone, letter, memorandum, e-mail, or fax depending on the audience, speed required, and formality.

4. The audience receives the message. But at this stage the sender does not know if it has been accepted and understood, or even received.

5. The audience does receive the message and decodes it to extract the idea in a form that is understood and has meaning. At this stage the sender can only hope that the message is correctly accepted as intended.

6. The audience replies with requested feedback enabling the sender to ascertain the effectiveness of the communication.

Managers have three basic responsibilities, according to Henry Mintzberg's *The Nature of Managerial Work*: to collect and disseminate information, to make decisions based on information, and to promote teamwork. Each is accomplished through effective communications. Besides memorandums, e-mails, reports, and phone calls, they often convey such information through meetings.

MANAGEMENT SKILLS

> *"Until someone has a small business, they have no comprehension of how hard it is. People, who start businesses from scratch, if they survive, are the toughest people on the face of the earth."*
> Sue Szymczak, Safeway Sling

A skill is the ability to translate knowledge and information into action that achieves a desired objective.

Three different kinds of managerial skills have been enumerated: technical, human, and conceptual. The requisite degree of each varies depending on the level in the management hierarchy.

- Technical skill is the ability to use the techniques, procedures, and tools of a specific field. This skill is particularly important at the first line of the organization where the manager needs to know how the work is done.
- Human skill is the ability to **communicate**, motivate, and lead individuals and groups. An understanding of human relations and organizational behavior is essential to managers in the middle ranks of management. These managers are concerned with directing lower-level supervisors and other middle managers therefore their jobs are more human than technical in nature. The ability to persuade, negotiate with, and coordinate the activities of others is the key to success.
- Conceptual skill is the ability to plan, coordinate, and integrate all of the organization's activities and interest. It is most important at the upper levels of the organization where long-range forecasting and planning are the principal activities.

Management is both an art and a science. As an art, management requires the use of behavioral and judgmental skills that cannot be quantified the way scientific information can.

Management is a science as well. It requires the use of logic and analysis. The manager arrives at a solution by observing, classifying, and studying facts. This scientific aspect of management has been enhanced by use of the computer and mathematical software.

When dealing with people, management is approach as an art; when dealing with things, it is approach as a science.

Successful managers will demonstrate the following skills:

- **Communication** – Good communication is the ability to deliver and share goals, ideas, and results clearly and concisely in both oral and written formats; and to receive information and feedback.
- Teamwork – Ability to be effective as a team leader and team member, able to participate in consensus building, conflict resolution, and negotiation.
- Self-Management – Ability to evaluate oneself, to modify behavior when necessary, and accomplish responsibilities and job obligations
- Leadership – Ability to motivate and support workers to achieved desired organizational goals

The manager's job is dynamic and ever changing. In *The Practice of Management*, Peter Drucker has articulated that "I'm not comfortable with the word *manager* anymore, because it implies subordinates." The rationale is that the manager today is a team leader, coordinator, coach, and facilitator more often than commander and a control person.

Managers today do more than the all-important planning, organizing, leading, and controlling. They also function in many roles for their organizations, such as:

- The figurehead role – they find that a considerable amount of time must be spent performing ceremonial duties.
- The leader role – they must always function as a leader, motivating, inspiring, and encouraging employees

- The liaison role – managers spent a lot of time in contact with others within and outside their organization.
- The spokesperson role – managers are often the voice of their organization to employees, customers, and vendors.
- The negotiator role – managers negotiate with suppliers, vendors, and unions.

Entrepreneurs as Communicators and Leaders

> *"The people who get on in this world are the people who get up and look for the circumstance they want, and, if they can't find them, make them."*
> George Bernard Shaw

Some 200 years ago the French Economist Jean Baptiste Say coined the term "Entrepreneur" from the French verb "Entrepredre", "To Undertake". The word "entrepreneur" has always eluded precise definition, but a pretty close definition is; "An Entrepreneur is someone who takes nothing for granted, assumes change is possible, and follows through; someone who is always thinking about ways to improve on the present reality; someone who believe that "A thought without action is nothing at all."

Leadership and communication is the pivotal force behind successful organizations. Both are necessary to help companies develop the vision of what they can be, and to mobilize the company toward that vision. Effective communication and good leadership is the process of influencing and motivating people to work together to achieve a common goal by helping them secure the knowledge, power, tools, and processes to do so.

What is Leadership? The question is simple, but the answer is not. Richard Barton, former CEO of Expedia, Inc. responds"

"I'll tell you what it is not. It's not management.

You have all these people with titles that have manager in it, and people talking about *management*. I hate the word. *Management is passive*. Management is minding the store. Management is something that you must do, that you don't necessarily enjoy doing. *Leadership* is leaning forward, looking ahead, trying to improve, being fired up about what you are doing and being able to communicate that, verbally and nonverbally, to those around you."

Leaders don't lean back, leaders lean forward.

Leadership is concerned with pointing the way. It is focused far more on the destination than on the details of getting there. Entrepreneurs must convey their vision of the firm's future to others in the business so that all involved can contribute to the accomplishment of the mission.

Although leaders must engage in some of the more mundane processes of management, particularly as the business grows, their first job is to create and communicate the vision.

Entrepreneurs are generally thought of as "Risk-Takers". Whereas it is true they do accept risk; those entrepreneurs who have realized the most success have proven to be the most conservative businessmen who constantly "hedge-their-bets" with every new venture. It is not solely being perceived as taking risk that defines an entrepreneur, but the willingness, even eagerness, to accept full responsibility for actions. That and the entrepreneur's vision of what can be and a strong faith in and persistent pursuit of that vision; coupled with the ability to motivate others to share in and work toward that vision. It is these attributes and traits that truly make an entrepreneur stand out as a leader.

Leadership skills were once thought of as a matter of birth. "Leaders were born, not made." This might be called the "Great Man" theory of leadership. A theory that even George Washington refuted stating: *"There are no great men, only great deeds."*

The Great Man theory sees power and leadership as being vested in a very limited number of people whose inheritance and destiny made them leaders. Either you had it, or you didn't. No amount of learning, experience, or desire could change your destiny. The Great Man theory view has failed to explain leadership. And with apologies to George Washington, so does the notion that great events make leaders out of otherwise ordinary people. Was he, Washington, simply on hand when the colonies decided to overthrow England and form a country? No, he had previously established himself as a leader of men, as a man of vision with the ability to inspire others to share in that vision.

Entrepreneurs are almost by definition leaders. Those to whom we have graced as great leaders of the past: George Washington, Moses, Julius Caesar, Alexander, Winston Churchill, etc., would in today's world and economy possess the potential to be great entrepreneurs. They would still be leaders of men inspiring and motivating others to follow their vision.

Now, as in the past, problems cannot be solved without successful organizations, and entrepreneur types invariably start organizations and those organizations cannot be successful without effective leadership. A business short of capital can borrow money, and one with a poor location can move. But a business short on leadership has little chance of survival. At best it will be left to the controls of efficient clerks, accountants, the "bean-counters".

Businesses must be led to overcome their inbred inertia of trained incapacity and to adapt to changing conditions. The entrepreneur's leadership is what gives the business its vision and its ability to translate that vision into reality. Without this translation, an exchange between leaders and followers, the business has no pulse, no heartbeat, and no life.

The problem with many companies, and especially the ones that are failing, is that they tend to be over-managed and under-led. They may master the ability to handle the daily routine, yet never question whether the routine should be done at all.

There is a profound difference between management and entrepreneur leadership: "To manage" means "to bring about, to accomplish, to have charge of or responsibility for, to conduct". "Leading" is "influencing, guiding in a direction, course, action, or opinion." The distinction is crucial. "Managers are people who do things right and leaders are people who do the right thing." The difference may be summarized as effectiveness - activities of vision and judgment versus efficiency - activities of mastering routines. For this reason, few managers are entrepreneurs and fewer entrepreneurs are managers. All entrepreneurs view themselves as leaders not bean-counters. They concern themselves with their company's basic purpose and general direction. Their perspective is vision-oriented. They see the forest not the trees. They do not spend their time with the nuts and bolts of the vision, but rather with accomplishing their vision, with doing the right thing.

A message published in the Wall Street Journal by United Technologies Corporation read:

"LET'S GET RID OF MANAGEMENT.

"You can dream, create, design, and build the most wonderful place in the world...but it requires people to make the dream a reality."
                                                                                    Walt Disney

People don't want to be managed. They want to be led.

Whoever heard of a World Manager? World Leader, yes; Educational Leader, Political Leader, Religious Leader, Community Leader, Labor Leader, Business Leader.

They lead. They don't manage.

You can lead your horse to water, but you can't manage him to drink.

If you want to manage someone, manage yourself. Do that well and you'll be ready to stop managing and start leading."

Entrepreneur leaders and non-entrepreneur leaders (government, military, religious, etc. - all whom could no doubt be great entrepreneurs if they so desire) all possess the same four types of people handling skills:

- **Vision**
- **Communication**
- **Trust**
- **Positive Self Image**

Entrepreneurs have consciously or subconsciously realized and captured these skills that are possessed by many but used by few. The skills can be learned by anyone, taught to everyone, and are denied to no one.

Only a few of us will be world leaders, but many of us as entrepreneurs will lead companies.

Vision:

Vision is the creating of focus. All entrepreneurs have urgency, an agenda, and an unparalleled concern with outcome. They are the most results-oriented people in the world. And since results get attention, their vision is compelling and draws others to them. Intensity together with commitment is magnetic and it pulls others to them. Vision grabs. Initially it grabs the entrepreneur and his persistence, commitment, and intensity grabs others to follow. Ray Kroc, founder of McDonalds, defined his vision as "a combination of background, instincts, and dreams."

Communication:

Walt Disney said, "If you can dream it, you can do it." We all will agree that entrepreneur/leader Walt Disney's dream (vision) has become a reality. Yet Mr. Disney idea is incomplete. Believing in one's dream is not enough. There are many people with lots of dreams, visions, and intentions, but without communications none will be realized. Success requires the capacity to communicate the vision, to induce enthusiasm and commitment in others. The very capacities possessed by the successful entrepreneur.

Followers rely upon the leader to define the reality of the vision they are asked to commit. Without this clarity of meaning, they feel the vision is blurry and indistinct; and they will not commit to it no matter how much the leader believes in it. He must convince them to share his vision, to commit and believe in it. The vision is not a reality to the followers until the entrepreneur convincingly communicates it. Like the baseball batter asking the umpire - Is it a strike or a ball? The umpire replies, *"It ain't nothing until I call it."* The leader must call it for his followers. His call is not simply communicating the facts; facts have to do with technique, but of his philosophy, his thinking about the vision. He prepares them for what is to be accomplished, and what ought to be done to accomplish it. It conveys the "know-why" ahead of the "know-how".

The key to this communication is *integrity* and *credibility*. Communication creates meaning for people. It's the only way any group can get behind the overall goals and vision of a business. Getting the message across is an absolute key. It is what distinguishes the entrepreneur as a leader.

Trust:

Trust is the lubrication that makes it possible for a business to work. It's hard to imagine a company without some semblance of trust operating. Trust applies accountability, predictability, and reliability. It's what sells products and keeps companies alive. Trust is the cement that holds a company's integrity. Effective internal communication greatly helps build employees trust. We trust entrepreneurs who are predictable, whose positions are known, and who keeps at it.

An entrepreneur fosters and relies upon the trust of his followers for he will involve the company and them in taking risk. It is important that his followers share in his vision and stay the course taking the risk with him. The persistence and determination of the entrepreneur must be conveyed to the people he is leading. They must trust in him to follow where he leads.

Positive Self Image:

Leadership is essential a human business and entrepreneurs/leaders work through others to accomplish their vision. To lead others, the management of self is critical. Without self-management and self-awareness, the leader does more harm than good to him and to others. This conveying of self makes leading a very personal affair. Therefore, a good feeling of self, a positive self-image is essential, and all good entrepreneurs have it. Positive self-regard is not extreme self-importance or egoistic self-centeredness. A true leader is not possessed with self-worship or cockiness. But they know their worth. They trust themselves without letting their ego get in the way. They have self-respect. Leaders display an inner strength and a constant set of values that everyone knows and can rely on. They avoid self-aggrandizement, inspire others, and exhibit a combination of modesty and extraordinary competence.

The successful entrepreneur/leader achieves a positive self-regard by recognizing strengths and compensating for weakness. He does not seek constant approval and recognition from outside of himself. It does not really matter how many people like him, but the quality of work resulting from his collaboration with them does. It is part of the leader's job to take risk, and risk cannot be pleasing to everyone.

Entrepreneurs/Leaders simply don't think about failure. "A mistake is just another way of doing things." Harry Truman would say. *"Whenever I make a bum decision, I just go out and make another one."*

The successful leader focuses on success, the fulfillment of his vision. Mrs. Wallenda recalls that when her husband, the great tightrope walker Karl Wallenda, fell to his death; All he thought about for three straight months prior was falling. It was the first time he ever thought about falling, always before he thought of nothing but walking the tightrope." It seemed to her that this time he put all his energy, his focus, into not falling rather than walking the tightrope.

Entrepreneurs/Leaders do not focus on failure. They even avoid the word - using instead such synonyms as: setback, mistake, false-start, and error, bum decision, etc. To focus on failure is to be destined to fail, to fall off the tightrope. Leaders focus on success, as do entrepreneurs.

When failure does occur, the successful entrepreneur uses it as a new beginning, an opportunity to regroup and refocus. *"If you not falling down, you not learning."*

Entrepreneurs quickly learn that successful leadership is a pull-style rather than a push- style. A pull style of influence works by attracting and energizing people to an exciting vision of the future. It motivates by identification rather than through rewards and punishments. They enroll themselves and others in the vision as attainable and worthy.

> *"If your actions inspire others to dream more, learn more, do more and become more, you are a leader."*
> John Quincy Adams

Leadership is an interpersonal influence exercised in a situation through **communication** to attain goals. These goals may be organizational, group or personal goals of the supervisor or the personal goals of the subordinate. The following conclusions define leadership further:

Leadership is a relationship

This relationship is based on position, power, ability, or some other factor,

The purpose of this relationship is to achieve some goal or objective,

The relationship involves individuals and groups,

In putting the relationship into practice, the organizational situation must be considered utilizing a variety of leadership styles.

In general, the term "leader" is interpreted by several meanings, but specifically in an organization, it means "management." The supervisory activity which is carried out by the person who oversees the problem solving and increases the productivity and progress of employees; It is the "management" role in business. To be an effective manager, one must have the leadership quality of self-confidence; confidence in decision making and, in the implementation, and follow through of those decisions.

Effective leadership involves working with employees to establish suitable, measurable, and reachable goals, action plans, and time lines. A good leader will be able to motivate people with the desire to achieve the goals. The leader/supervisor delegates and provides ongoing guidance and support as the employees complete the desired action plan. Rarely can success be accomplished without the leader's consideration for other aspects of the employees' life, e.g., time dedicated to training, career preferences, and personal strengths and weakness, as well as a balanced personal life. Subsequently a leader is often confronted with a fine line between being a supervisor and a personal confident.

The Entrepreneur Process

> *"If everything seems under control, you're just not going fast enough."*
> Mario Andretti

During an earlier banking career, a former customer and business-owner advised that he did not know how to spell entrepreneur, nor did he know what it meant, but everyone said that he was one. He was without formal education, but he was a master at his business. An expert in the petrochemical industry with much hands-on technical skill, a dynamic motivator of employees with excellent pragmatic communication skills, and a true leader who was always able to clearly enumerate the objectives before his company and to have others share in the vision of achieving the goal. He was a good communicator to those within and without the company.

From the conception of the business idea, he and other entrepreneurs followed the entrepreneurial process to become a successful owner-manager by starting, growing, and managing a profitable business. They all had a strong passion for the business with targeted focus on their customers and products/services; demonstrating unfailing persistence and tenacity in pursuit of their vision.

That entrepreneurial process through which a new venture is created, and an existing venture is sustained is as follows:

- The decision to become an entrepreneur; to be their own boss and work for themselves, to pursue their own ideas, and to realize the financial rewards
- The development of a successful business idea, to recognize and seize the opportunity, to generate feasibility ideas from industry and competitor analysis, and to develop an effective business model
- Taking the steps to move from an idea to an entrepreneurial firm, taking the calculated risks and building a new venture team; writing, rewriting, and revisiting the Business Plan, assessing the new ventures financial strengths, viability and sources of funding; overcoming adversity
- Managing and growing the entrepreneurial firm to maturity while maintaining the entrepreneur spirit, innovation, and culture with constant emphasis on the five "Ps" of marketing success (People, Product, Price, Promotion, and Place).

There is no one or simple definition of what an entrepreneur is; most would agree that it is someone who recognizes a marketing opportunity, assembles the resources to seize the opportunity with a willingness to accept the risk in pursuing the vision to create something of value and reap the reward for the effort and sacrifices. Someone with the ability and talent to convince others to join in the effort either with their energy, time, talent, and capital to share in making the dream a reality; the entrepreneur is an innovative visionary with effective communication skills to motivate others to share the vision and endure the sacrifices to reap the ultimate harvest of personal and financial satisfaction.

Surprisingly there are many that answer this call; many seeking opportunity for financial independence, monetary rewards, the recognition and accolades of others, and personal satisfaction. Some with well-planned efforts, carefully thought-out and researched, others, rather carelessly, with little thought toward the feasibility of the vision or to the capital requirements to reach fulfillment of the venture and with what to do, how to manage, if success is realized.

Those that start a business with little regard with managing and growing that business, with dangerous inconsideration for all who may follow, join, or do business with the venture is not an entrepreneur but an opportunist. A few do so quite deliberately to seize a momentary personal reward no matter whom else may be hurt, but most are well-intentioned and simply not aware of the difficulties and pitfalls ahead, nor the management and people skills needed to succeed. Failure, often perplexing failure, is the usual result. Quickly the entrepreneur must realize that if this vision is to become a reality, if the venture is to grow profitably with the ability to sustain itself, management skills and a talented team must be acquired.

As a rule, entrepreneurs normally do not have the resources to launch an enterprise. They must convince others to participate with money, time, effort, talent, and commitment. To solicit others to join in and to believe in their vision requires some of the management skills and traits necessary to grow and operate the venture. Most notably are **communication skills** and traits of trust, honesty, and integrity.

All the boring skills that by the entrepreneur's very nature are contrary to his reason for going into business, to his personality and thinking, are required. He must obtain a working knowledge of them and must surround himself with those who can complement him with these abilities. Besides the technical skill of the industry entered, which usually all entrepreneurs possess, are the following:

- **Writing and Oral Communication**
- Business Management
- Time Management
- Listening
- Ability to Organize
- Network Building
- Coaching
- Planning and Goal Setting
- Economic Awareness

- Decision-Making
- Marketing
- Finance
- Accounting
- Negotiation
- Cash-Flow Management
- Business Ethics
- Growth Management
- Leadership
- Persistence
- Innovation
- Flexibility
- Self-Discipline, Awareness, and Control

Michael E. Gerber has written *The E-Myth: Why Most Businesses Don't Work and What to Do About It*. He delineates the differences among the types of persons involved with small businesses:

- The entrepreneur creates a business that can work without him. He is a visionary who makes the business unique by imbuing it with a special and exciting sense of purpose, direction and vision. The entrepreneur's far-reaching perspective enables him to anticipate changes and needs in the market and to initiate action to capitalize on them.
- The manager produces results through employees by developing and implementing effective systems and, by interacting with and supporting employees, enhances their self-esteem and abilities to produce the desired results. The manager actualizes the entrepreneur's vision through planning, motivation, implementation, and analysis.
- The technician performs specific tasks according to systems and standards management developed. The technician not only gets the work done but also provides input to supervisors for improvement of those procedures.

Gerber contends that most small business *"don't work, their owners do."* He believes that today's small business owner works too hard at a job that he has created for himself rather than working to create a business. Thus, most small businesses fail because the owner is more of a "technician" than an "entrepreneur" working in the business rather than on the business.

The E-Myth is that today's business owners are not true entrepreneurs who create businesses but merely technicians who now have created a job for themselves. The solution to the myth lies in the owner's willingness to begin thinking and acting like a true entrepreneur: to imagine how the business would work without him. In addition to working in the business, the owner must begin to work on the business.

The entrepreneur launching a new venture and growing an existing business must be achievement oriented and customer driven, enjoys taking control of his/her own destiny and assumes responsibility for their decisions. They usually dislike repetitive routine tasks but do enjoy a challenge. They are persistent in their pursuit with much energy and imagination to see what others cannot. They are willing and comfort with moderate calculated risk which they can perceive as being transform into the dream they aspire to create no matter how intangible it may appear to others. Most importantly, through learned skills or natural charisma, they know how to inspire and lead others to join in their quest.

CHAPTER ONE

GOALS AND FOUNDATIONS

"You can't direct the wind, but you can adjust the sails."

In any communication there is a Sender and a Receiver.

Effective communication dictates that the message is understood by the receiver and that it stimulates action. Good communication is the ability to deliver and share goals, ideas, and results clearly and concisely in both oral and written formats; and to receive information and feedback.

Communicate comes from the Latin word *communicare* meaning "to share." So, it follows that the goal of any communication is to share information to accomplish a specific objective, solicit cooperation, motivate toward an acceptable action, or simply understanding and agreement.

In all communication consideration must be made to select the right media to convey your message. A media is the form through which you choose to transmit your message for the maximum effect and reception to proper parties. Analyze your audience and decide if oral, written, or electronic will be the best media.

ORAL

Oral consist of face-to-face, either one-on-one or in meetings, large and small, speeches, and presentations. Oral contacts enable valuable instant feedback to help assure clarity and understanding.

WRITTEN

A written message can be as informal as an internal memorandum of a formal letter within or without the organization. This media is best when retention of the document and information is essential.

ELECTRONIC

This media is fast replacing all others for it speed and convenience. It combines both oral and written in a visual manner. Oral visual medias can be by telephone, teleconferences, voice-mail, and the ever-increasing use of e-mail.

GOALS:

RECEIVER UNDERSTANDING – The receiver understands the message as the sender intends.

This is the most important goal of business communication-receiver understanding. Without understanding there is no communication.

RECEIVER RESPONSE- The receiver provides the necessary response to the sender (feedback).

FAVORABLE RELATIONSHIP- The sender and the receiver maintain a favorable relationship.

ORGANIZATIONAL GOODWILL- The sender's organization gains/ maintains goodwill.

It is important to strive to achieve these goals (as it always has been) due to the speed and rapid changes in technology dispersing information (internet, voicemail, fax, etc.) resulting in an ever-changing age of data. We often work with and within teams and coworkers requiring rapid exchanging of information and assurance that all are up-to-date. We also have a very diverse culture and are engage in Global Business making dispersion of information and its understanding vitally important.

SENDER'S ROLE:

Analyze the receiver – by an awareness of their knowledge, education, experience, and vocabulary level; by their interest, concerns, needs, and motivation; by their attitudes, values, opinions, biases, and viewpoints.

Select message type and channel

> Use the "you-viewpoint"; put yourself in their position and understanding level to assure you are communicating in a manner that will be well received and understood.
>
> Provide for feedback; without feedback the sender does not know if the message has been received and understood.
>
> Remove communication barriers; all that may prevent the reception and understanding of the message.

RECEIVER'S ROLE:

> Listen or read carefully to assure understanding
> Be open to different senders and new ideas
> Make notes when necessary
> Provide appropriate feedback
> Ask questions for clarification
> There are six steps in the communication process, three for the sender and three for the receiver:

SENDER:

> Has an idea (message/information) to send
>
> Encodes that idea in an understandable manner
>
> Send the idea in an appropriate way

RECEIVER:

> Receives the message
>
> Decodes the message for understanding
>
> Provides feedback

Communication is simply the process of sending and receiving information, whether with customers, vendors, investors, bankers, superiors, mentors, and exceedingly important, with employees. The ability to motivate and inspire all stakeholders is priceless for the entrepreneur soon learns that to achieve success requires others with a concerted effort. No matter how resourceful and self-reliant the individual entrepreneur is, maximum results with best be achieved with a team-effort. This ability to communicate and convey shared values and goals is a trademark of those who have learned that <u>it is essential to work on the business and not simply in the business.</u>

As you progress in your business and/or rise in your organization more and more does communication becomes more important. The entrepreneur will find him/herself devoting increasingly higher percentage of time communicating with others.

Employees/subordinates and even superiors, vendors, creditors, and investors will all expect you to:

- $ Organize information coherently and clearly
- $ Express and present information succinctly and persuasively
- $ Listen effectively
- $ Communicate successfully with people from diverse backgrounds
- $ Familiar with the various communication technology
- $ Communicate in an etiquette civilized manner
- $ Communicate ethically

Miscommunication resulting in a chaotic effort with always result in failure of the desired goal.

The basic goal is to get others to do what you want them to do in a mutually beneficial manner. Most will be moved to do something if the perceive the potential for personal gain. Your power to persuade will depend on this ability to stir that motivation.

People respond to incentives.

Therefore:

- know your audience and learn their motives and interest, find the right motive and people will persuade themselves
- if problems or obstacles, attack them and not the people, separate people from the problem and never be negative or hostile. Positive motivation works
- give your audience respect and in return get respect

- always look for the common ground and shared values to establish a rapport
- use a step-by-step, persuasive sequence; desired action is seldom achieved in one step; attention must be obtained, understanding must be achieved, and emotions must be aroused.

CHAPTER TWO

MEETINGS AND TEAMS

"God so loved the world that He did not send a committee."

The bane of but ever-increasing necessity of doing business is the meeting. Utilized with greater frequency in formal and informal settings to advance information and motivate group effort.

Team formation is a large component of corporate structure for assurance of efficiency and understanding in the successful accomplishment of the desired outcome. Team communication offers some relief for management in that problems and actions can be worked out among employees. They are usually short-lived task forces or problem-solving teams to resolve specific situations or imminent goals. For longer term resolution formal committees are established on a permanent basis to handle recurring situations and provide oversight of total operations and progress (or lack of).

"No man is an island. No man stands alone."
John Donne

Teams and meetings are a distinct part of participative management involving employees in the decision-making process. They share the mission and are each responsible for the joint efforts. Because employees are participating in the decision process, they are committed to seeing it succeed. They are instrumental in creativity, productivity, conflict resolution, and efficiency while enhancing employee morale. An effective functioning team can combine resources, knowledge, and experience to contribute to the desired result.

However, there is the possibility of poorly managed unsuccessful teams and meetings that would waste value time and money, reduce work efficiency and quality, and frustrate both management and employees. They must strive to avoid the negative impact of groupthink, hidden agendas, and wasted expense. A primary reason for this outcome is poor communication and the flow of vital information in a timely and understandable manner. Clear understandability communication will assure a common-purpose in resolution.

Contributing to this problem are often standing committees that have outlived their original purpose but continue to meet. In all situations management and team leaders must be mindful of the potential for peer pressure, group thinking, and hidden agendas of attendees which would undermined any success.

In today's business, meetings are the primary means of communications whether they are formally or informally held even if virtually conducted on the internet. Well-run meetings can help to keep everyone on the same page in the organization's effort, and help to solve problems, conflicts, develop ideas, identify opportunities, and provide a forum of employee feedback. Preparation for the meeting and the manager's communication and listening skill are paramount for successful outcomes. Poorly run meetings waste value management and employee time costing thousands of dollars.

Unfortunately, most meetings do not go well. From your own meeting attendance, the norm seems to be boring, uninforming, uninteresting, not necessary, baffling, or just a colossal waste of time. Since modern management is striving for a participating form, meetings are increasing. A good meeting will get the job done, but too often it is not clear what the job is. Most lack effective participation and even proper management and leadership. Leadership does not mean dominating the discussion and the participants but organizing the agenda and balancing the discussion for a consensus outcome and solution resulting in an achievable action-plan.

Meetings usually come in three kinds: the "ritual meeting", the "planning ahead" meeting, and the "things-are-gone-to-hell" meeting.

Ritual meetings exist because they have always existed and are for -the-most part ceremonial. The Monday morning or Friday afternoon meeting usually with the same agenda and issues in which nothing is ever resolved. But people do come together and discuss their weekend, drink coffee, but other than so comradeship, nothing is accomplished for the organization. It is a shame, for these times are wasted opportunities or simply a costly waste of time. There are a lot of ritual meetings in aging business, banks, and universities. These ritual meetings look very active, and things seem to happen. Problems are identified and prioritized and then no action is taken. The agenda and order for the next meeting is the same with no proposed solutions for identified problems.

Planning Ahead meetings are usually better prepared and not as regular. There is an agenda which is distributed beforehand, and although there is time allocated for new ideas, they usually start on time and end on time.

Things-are-going-to-Hell meetings are usually conducted to ask why things are going to hell and what can we do about it. They are difficult to conduct with everyone wanting to talk at once to give excuses or their point of view. The reason for this type of meeting is usually because people did not do what they were supposed to or promised to do. Sometimes there may be an unexpected reason for the problem. The ability to communicate in language understood by all participants is vital if the difficulty is to be addressed. Miscommunication and different understanding by the participants will not solve the problem.

Unfortunately, many meetings are unproductive, accomplishing nothing, and a waste of time. Senior management may spend half of its time in meetings with middle manager averaging a third of their work hours. Despite the current technology of conference calls, e-mail, fax, cell phones, internet meetings, most organizations are still running by inefficient, unnecessary meetings accounting for anywhere from 10% to 20% of personnel cost.

So how can managers make meetings more effective and productive? They should utilize the **four "P's" of effective meeting preparation: Purpose, Planning, Participants, and Process.**

Purpose: Should this meeting be held? Why hold it? Can the objective be communicated some other way? If the information can be communicated by e-mail, phone, and memo, other than a pep-talk gathering, the cost of the meeting exceeds the potential rewards, and then the meeting should not be held. The objective of the meeting should be defined, and the agenda disseminated in advance. To have a productive and effective meeting will required a thought-out action-oriented agenda in the planning step.

Planning: refers to the preparation of the agenda. Items to be covered should be put in order of importance, or some other structure such as announcements, committee reports, old and new business. The time to be allocated for each should be indicated and followed. This will help to keep on schedule and to end on time. The meeting's agenda should be plan in every detail, who (will attend), what (will be discussed), where (where will it be held), when (at with time and day), and why (purpose).

Participants: attendance should be limited to those people concerned with the topics on the agenda. The more people at the meeting, especially those with no purpose for being there, the longer the discussions destroying time management and creating the potential for unrelated bull and a longer unproductive meeting. Some participants should only be invited to that part of the meeting that they have an interest and can contribute.

Process: refers to the actual conducting of the meeting to assure that it is effective. The appropriate time and place must be choosing; lighting, size, tables and chairs, audio-visual aids, and refreshments are all important. Distribute the minutes of the last meeting, and the present agenda and other material ahead of time sufficient for them to read in advance. This prevents the waste of time of reading during the meeting. Bring extra copies to the meeting for those who may forget theirs. A day or two prior to the meeting have reminders sent out as to the time and place. Close the meeting by summarizing the decisions reached, tasks assigned, progress accomplished, and key points discussed. Review action plans that will be reported upon at the next meeting.

DURING THE MEETING

Keeping control, providing leadership and direction during the meeting can prove to be more difficult than preparing for the meeting. Good preparation will certainly assist in an effective meeting, and the following six ways will also:

1. Start on time. Give warning when the meeting will begin and stick to it. People will arrive on time if the meeting starts on time. Discourage tardiness by having the minutes of the last meeting reflect those present, absent, or late.

2. Start with the predistributed agenda and stick with it. Put and enforce a time limit of appropriate importance on each topic.

3. An introduction before handing out related materials can save time of participants scanning prior to directing their attention to the items.

4. Try to involve everyone in attendance. If the meeting was properly planned they all belong there and should have something to contribute.

5. Review all results, decisions, accomplishments, and actions for the next meeting. This is a good time to set the time and place for that meeting if required.

6. End on time.

Everyone in a meeting, leader and participants share the responsibility for successful meetings. However, if you have called the meeting and are the leader, you have an extra degree of responsibility and accountability for a productive meeting. A good meeting leader will strive to stay on track as per the agenda. The leader may stimulate the participants by guiding, probing, and mediating them with occasional summarize what is being discussed and the ongoing conclusions. The leader will know when to push forward or step back to let others talk; after all they are there to participate. There will also be times to stop discussion when time is being wasted to stay on schedule.

To assure staying on track, it will be helpful to follow previous agreed upon rules and agenda. Formal meetings always use parliamentary procedure which can be found in *Roberts Rules of Order*. But even informal meetings are best served by following a clear set of rules that all are familiar with.

To gather new ideas and information derived from the experience and knowledge of participants, they must be encouraged to participate. As the meeting progresses, some will remain too quiet while others will be too talkative dominating the allotted time. Draw out the reticent members who may simply not be paying attention, are shy, or expressing disagreement by their silence by asking direct questions of them. For the overly talkative, advise that time is limited and we all want to hear from others.

If you are a participant, then do participate by trying to contribute to the topic being discussed to help achieve the meeting's purpose goals. Speak up if you have something constructive to say, but don't monopolize the discussion.

As a participant, you may cringe at attending. What could be more boring or a waste of your time, as well as that of your organizations, then being forced to listen to a wind-bag in authority. Yet, meetings could very well be helpful in advancing your career for you will have the attention of senior management and this could be an opportunity to shine. It can just as easily break your career advancement hopes by demonstrating your lack of knowledge, understanding, or communication skills.

Ten things **never** to do in a meeting:

1. Be Late – Walking into a meeting already in progress indicates how disorganized, undisciplined, and disrespectful you are of your boss's and coworker's time.

2. Be Unprepared - Your time to shine. If you have been given an agenda and material beforehand, read them. Prepare any questions, comments, or contributions you may make.

3. Monopolize the Conversation – It is always wise to let more senior people contribute first. Once they have finished, concisely and succinctly make your points. Don't feel compel to speak at all if you don't have anything material or purposeful to say. It has been said, "Better to be thought a fool, then speak and remove all doubt."

4. Make Your Statements Sound Like Questions - Phrasing your statements like questions invites others to say "no", "argue" or "take credit" for your ideas.

5. Misread Signals – Try to gauge the needs and mood of the meeting. Listen carefully to what is being said to ascertain how receptive your ideas and comments will be in accordance with the meeting's purpose.

6. Get Intimidated – Some regard meetings as war fighting to get the boss's attention. If you are put-down, calmly defend yourself and your ideas.

7. Chew Gum – Nothing is more annoying than the smacking, popping, and cracking of chewing gum. It's rude and unprofessional.

8. Keep Your Cell Phone On – Hopefully, you turn it off in church, restaurants, and the movies. Turn it off in the meeting. A ringing phone interrupts the presenter and distracts the audience. And never take a call or make a call while in a meeting. This too, is rude and unprofessional.

9. Wander Off Topic – Don't abandon the agenda to discuss something else which may be of more interest to you.

10. Skip It – If the meeting was called, especially by senior management, attend. Sure, you might rationalize that you will get more done by not wasting the meeting time. But you may miss some pertinent information. Remember, it could be your time to shine. Meetings aren't always about productivity, most are a waste of time, and therefore, for you it may be about projecting a positive image and forming the relationships that will be essential to your career success.

AFTER THE MEETING

Meeting minutes should be prepared and distributed within 24 hours. Prepare all progress reports and insure that all action decisions are carried out. Review the progress of various established committees and abolish those committees which have accomplished their purpose and are no longer necessary.

LISTENING

To be a truly good communicator, you must do more than improve your oral and written sending skills; you must also improve your receiving (listening) skills. To succeed in business and the ability to motivate and lead others, you must be an effective listening. Nothing will enhance the trust an employee has with management then management willingness to listen effectively to their viewpoint and ideas. Organizations with good up and down communications, requiring true listening from both, usually reach their objective and goals. All stay informed, aware, interested, current, and move toward common achievements. Conversely, poor listening skills on the part of managers and employees can substantially increase cost, create mistakes, and impede accomplishments.

The listening process involves five steps: receiving, interpreting, remembering, evaluating, and responding.

1. Receiving: Physically hearing the message and acknowledging it
2. Interpreting: Assign meaning to what is heard
3. Remembering: Store the information for future use
4. Evaluating: Evaluate the information
5. Responding: React based on what you have heard and understood

The evaluation step is crucial. You must listen actively with focus attention to comprehend and structure what is being conveyed. Realize that your mind can process information faster than the speaker can send it; therefore, you must focus on what is being said less you become distracted.

Also strive to avoid prejudgment. We all have experience, values, and beliefs which may influence our acceptance of what is being said. Selective perceptions can distort the information to fit what we already believe about the subject. Try to listen with an open mind to digest any new information or another viewpoint.

Ask yourself:

- What am I being asked to do?
- What are they leading up to?
- Why am I being asked to do it?
- What is my motive, what are the speaker's motives?
- When am I supposed to do this and on what schedule?
- Why am I listening to this?
- Who is it important to?

The remembering step can prove difficult and is easily dismissed during a meeting. If the information is to be retained, do not rely on your memory. Record it in some fashion even if simply taking casual written notes.

Effective listening also requires mastering using silence productively. Learn to handle silence so you are not forced into a premature half-thought response. Silence in itself is communication.

NONVERBAL COMMUNICATION

In managing and leading others, it is not often what is being said but what is perceived that has an impact on performance. In this regard nonverbal communications play a huge part, too often for the negative for it is usually done without forethought and instinctively. In a positive connotation, nonverbal communication should be used to reinforce the spoken message. Nonverbal communication is the process of sending and receiving information, both intentionally and unintentionally, without using written or spoken language. Nonverbal gestures and facial expressions can strengthen a verbal message when they match and compliment the words. They can undermine and weaken the verbal message when they don't match the words or, in some cases, replace the unspoken word.

Nonverbal communication may often convey more than the sender intended than the words spoken. Nonverbal signals include facial expressions, gestures and posture, vocal characteristics, personal appearance, touch, time and personal space. Posture and body movements can signal your energy level, and your openness and receptiveness to an idea, or your closeness and resistance to it. Open body position is revealed in leaning forward with uncrossed arms and legs. Closed or defense body position include leaning back, sometimes with both arms and legs crossed or close together, or even hands in pockets. Notice your own body the next time you are speaking to a friend. You will naturally assume an open body position. Notice your next business meeting, you may observe that many adopt a closed posture indicated that they may be slightly uncomfortable.

- Facial Expressions – The face is the primary tool we all use to express emotion most often instinctively unless practiced (which is usually recognized and ineffective). Your eyes, called the windows of the soul, are especially effective in indicating

your mood, attention, interest, influencing and motivating others, and true feelings.
- Gestures and Posture – The art and ability to use gesture can be most effective in reinforcing a point. By movement you can express both specific and general messages, some intentionally some not. Slouching, leaning forward, fidgeting, wandering around, and walking briskly are all usually unconscious actions but may indicate whether you feel confident or nervous, friendly or hostile, in agreement or not, assertive or passive, powerful or powerless.
- Vocal Characteristics – The tone of your voice, like your face, carries intentional and unintentional messages of your true feelings. Your voice can reveal things which you may be unaware. Your volume, the inflection, speaking pace, and the little annoying "ums" and "ahs" that creep into your message, all indicate your confidence level, sincerity, your relationship with the listeners, knowledge, background, and emotions.
- Personal Appearance – People will judge you and your professionalism by your appearance, fairly or unfairly. Few of us can control our physical appearance and such is usually not suspect; but we are able to control our grooming, clothing, and accessories. We should know our audience and dress appropriately to impress, influence and be accepted favorably.
- Touch – Touch is valuable in conveying warmth, comfort, and reassurance. Touch is powerful and best left for personal relationships. Touch is a complex tool and usual not best use in a professional setting. When in doubt, don't touch.
- Time and Space – Like touch, time and especially space can be used to assert authority, imply intimacy, and send other nonverbal messages. You show respect by being on time; disrespect and disregard for others by making people wait (often a tactic to assert one's own importance). As with touch, standing too close, invading someone's private space, can be a violation or a sign of sincere emotion.

When attending a meeting as a listener, look for and pay attention to the speaker's nonverbal clues to receive the whole message. Do they enhance and reinforce the spoken words, or do they contradict them? Be observant but don't assume that your observations are infallible. If you feel that there is a contradictory message being sent from the words and the gesture, respectfully ask for clarification or explore further.

When presenting at a meeting be attentive of some of the following to determine if you are holding or losing the audience:

- Scratching the head indicating confusion or disbelief
- Biting the lips indicating anxiety
- Rubbing the back of the head and neck suggesting frustration, impatience
- Avoiding eye contact indicating a lack of interest
- Crossing of arms indicating resistance, defensiveness, defiance, or a close mind
- Sighing and yawning, a sign of boredom

WRITTEN BUSINESS COMMUNICATION

Whether writing a simple memorandum, e-mail, or a more complex report or presentation, you must be aware of the recipient and their understanding of the message to initiate the desired action. To communicate effectively, you must create a message that is concise, succinct, with a clear understandable purpose. There is a three-step writing process to create effective business messages in any form that is chosen as most appropriate.

It is **planning**, **writing**, and **completing** the business message.

Planning - as with analyzing any situation, you must define your purpose and the intended audience. Make sure that the information being communicated is understandable by the audience for if not understood, it won't be communicated. Select the proper medium to transmit the message – written (e-mail, memorandum, letter), or oral. Organize the information, limiting your scope to the main idea to be accomplished; an outline may help in organization.

Writing - after planning and organizing the message, make sure that it will fit the audience, their language skills, sensitivities, and style. Compose the message using direct, clear language with familiar words and short concise paragraphs. This is an opportunity to build further rapport with your audience, and enhance credibility, trust, and loyalty. Be mindful of their values and polite and respectful in your tone.

Completing – review and revise the message (if necessary) prior to sending. Make sure that it has a professional appearance, is readable, clear, concise, and correct, and that it is being distributed to all interested parties. Produce and proofread the message for sloppy typos, misspellings, grammar, and other errors; all which will destroy your credibility and purpose.

More than likely your short messages will be by electronic means rather than hard-copy paper memorandums. Today businesses are using instant messages, texting, and blogging, as well as e-mail. However, most will be by e-mail which has replaced the printed memo and letter. No doubt you have much experience with e-mail but always be mindful that e-mail correspondence at work is considerably different than your personal e-mail communications. They are more formal than those you send to family and friends. Be sure to handle it as a professional business communication, follow your established company policy and culture. For clarity of purpose, always use a concise relative subject line and use proper language in the body of the message. Avoid slang and of course obscenities. When replying to a group e-mail, be sure to reply only to the sender and not to all (if that is the intent).

E-mail etiquette in accordance with company policy and norms is essential. Before composing and sending make sure that the e-mail is necessary and that it does not contribute to the overabundance of e-mails received every day. To not do so with relegate your e-mails to the superfluous and considered a waste-of-time damaging your professionalism and credibility.

SOME TIPS FOR EFFECTIVE E-MAIL

When requesting information or action, make it clear what you are asking for, why it's important, and when you need it. Try not to make your reader write back for these details. People will be tempted to ignore your messages if they are not clear about what you want or when you want it.

When replying to an e-mail, paraphrase the request to remind the reader what you are replying to.

If possible, avoid sending long, complex e-mails. A long complex message is better communicated as a printed memorandum or report.

Know your audience and adjust the formality of the language. Overly formal messages to peers and colleagues are perceived as stuffy and distant; too informal language to superiors and customers are perceived as disrespectful.

NEVER TYPE THE E-MAIL IN CAPS. All caps are perceived as shouting and screaming.

Don't annoy your reader with cutesy formatting, colors, or unusual fonts.

Don't compose and send an e-mail when angry. E-mails can be forwarded anywhere and saved forever. Don't let poor judgment ruin your career and reputation.

Many consider the "return receipt request" feature an annoyance and an invasion of privacy. Only use it for the most critical messages.

Don't infect anyone with a computer virus. Make sure you have a current virus protection on your computer.

Always pay attention to grammar, spelling, and capitalization. Just because it is an e-mail, do not abandon the etiquette of proper professional communication. Do not succumb to the computer language of adolescents. As your personal appearance and dress says something about you, so does the appearance of your e-mail.

Whether in an e-mail message, a written memorandum, or a more formal business report, you may encounter two commonly used abbreviations which we have all seen but often confuse or simply do not know what they mean.

They are *i.e.* and *e.g.*

The abbreviation *i.e.* stands for the Latin *id est,* meaning "that is" (The parcel exceeds the weight limit, *i.e.* three pounds).

The abbreviation *e.g.* stands for the Latin *exempli gratia,* meaning "for the sake of example" or "for example" (The management may provide an incentive, *e.g.,* a cash bonus or time off).

REDUNDANCES

To assure clear concise communication, the sender whether orally or written, should avoid repetitiveness, verbosity, and wordiness. Don't repeat yourself other than for emphasis in a summary. For instance, "large in size" is redundant because what else is large but a size. Or avoid "past experience" or "actual experience"- you can't experience something in the future, and you can't experience something if it doesn't exist.

Other examples follow:

Absolute complete	complete
Basic fundamentals	fundamentals
Check up on	check
Disappear from sight	disappear
Each and every	each
Few in number	few
Hopeful optimism	optimism
Important essentials	essentials
Joint cooperation	cooperation
Mix together	mix
New innovation	innovation
One and the same	the same
Period of time	period
Repeat again	repeat
Same identical	same
Total of ten	ten
Unsolved problem	problem

CHAPTER THREE

THE BUSINESS PLAN

"An action without thought is nothing, and a thought without action is nothing at all."

One of the most important communication tools, written, oral, and visual presentation, for an entrepreneur is composing and delivering the Business Plan.

Seeking money becomes a never-ending quest for the small business owner. Either there is not enough to start with, but the undaunted enterpriser persists anyway due to unrealistic ambitions or ignorance to what is needed to launch the new venture, or the well-capitalized business owner launches without a plan and quickly burns through start-up capital, or a well-thought out venture that enjoys relative but unanticipated success finds that existing funds are rapidly becoming scarce before positive cash flow can be internally generated; in all situations when the solutions is to seek money from others a plan is required.

So, is the sole or primary purpose of a Business Plan being to raise capital? Does not every lender, investor, and even trade creditors want to see one? Why?

Although this written communication and presentation may be about raising money and the Business Plan is referred to as being essential in that endeavor; raising money is not the paramount reason a serious prospective or existing small business owner should have one.

$ENTREPRENEUR COMMUNICATION$

Would you consider undertaking a road trip to an unknown destination without consulting a roadmap? Some would and those that would will have more difficulty than those that would not. It has been determined that within 10 years as much as 75% to 80% of all new small business ventures fail due to lack of proper management.

The textbook definition of management functions is planning, organizing, controlling, and leading. Too many entrepreneurs have great difficulty in transitioning from entrepreneur and business founder to on-going entrepreneur and business manager.

They forget or discount the planning aspects of running a business and concentrate on the building of the business, the sales, the networking, the fun parts of the business, the reasons why they went into business in the first place. The entrepreneur that does not soon learn that for the business to survive it must be run like a business with attention to details and not ran as a hobby.

A good entrepreneur must become a good business manager and leader not only for himself, but also for the customers, employees, investors, and creditors. Those business owners that are quick to point out that they are too busy building and working in the business will discover that the business is not being worked on, not being developed and nurtured.

The entrepreneur will state that there is no time for deliberation and planning, much less to put a business plan in writing, besides "the plan is in my head, I have no time for fairy-tale projections into the future, if the present is not handled there will be no future". This is a typical attitude of the business owner who is more of an opportunist than entrepreneur. An entrepreneur is not simply a person that starts a business and takes reckless risk; a true entrepreneur starts, grows, and manages a business after due deliberations of accepting the calculated risk in exploring the business concept and identifying market possibilities in a for-profit venture. Without the discipline of planning, forethought, anticipation of expenses and realistic expectations of sales and cash flow management, the would-be business owner is like a child learning to ride a bicycle, frantically striving not to fall by pedaling faster and faster. Fall they will; it usually does not become a situation of will they fail, but when they will fail.

Inadvertently those opportunistic entrepreneurs that lack the internal locus-of-control of **"If it's going to be it is up to me"** and are not

THE BUSINESS PLAN

purpose commitment to a specific venture will blame the failure on outside forces such as lack of capital, lack of sales acceptance, too much competition, a poor location, and not enough help. All of which are symptoms of the problem not the cause which is the lack of planning and management ability which are the real causes for the difficulties and business failures.

Therefore, while a Business Plan is needed and used to raise capital, it must first and always be used as a dynamic planning tool serving the entrepreneur himself as a feasibility plan for the business concept. An idea for a business is not a concept of a business model but only the beginning of one. The plan must first communicate to the planner before others.

Launching a new venture does have an element of risk. The new business alone may not be inherently risky, but the unprepared and uninitiated entrepreneur is the risk. The prepared new business owner would have first planned to minimize the risk to a calculated one. A business plan for establishing and determining the feasibility of the venture and the entrepreneur's fit. It would have been prepared to answer such question as:

- Does the entrepreneur have the personal skills, knowledge, expertise, perseverance, desire, and mindset to launch a new venture?
- Is there a target market for the proposed product, service, and business being contemplated?
- Can the market be reached and how and what resources will be needed?
- What resources are available to sustain the business until it can surpass the breakeven point and sustain itself?
- Where will those resources come from?
- How long will it take to reach breakeven?
- Will other employees be needed and when and with what skills and abilities?
- From where and how can the business attract those key employees and at what cost?
- At what price will the product be offered, is it competitive?
- Will the profit margin be sufficient to support overhead and produce a profit?

- Who will be the business' vendors and suppliers and at what cost and terms will the business be able to purchase?
- How dependent will the business be upon those vendors and trade creditors and are there any other sources in the event of interruption?

Depending on the industry and the entrepreneur's background and personal situation there could many other different questions which a thorough business plan will help to determine before an individual mistakenly invest personal and other resources and time into a venture that has no practical expectation of success. A plan that determines that a venture is unwise would have serve its purpose and done its job of advising and forewarning the entrepreneur. It should and could reveal other entrepreneurial opportunities that would work and pay that are more reasonable to pursue.

The new business owner may be from the legion of "reluctant entrepreneurs"; those many thousands that for various reason have found themselves out of a job. We have seen too many laid off, downsized, outsized, fired who feel displaced and are anxious to get back into the game. The desire may be strong, but the motivation could be misdirected. If they were fortunate to have been separated from their employment with a pension or savings to invest; this very ease of entry into something may be a downfall and lead to losing the savings. A thorough study and a plan will be necessary to reduce the possibility of lost and to determine the reluctant entrepreneur's expectations.

The attraction of being independent, the freedom of being one's own boss, the drive to work for self and reap the rewards of your own efforts is strong and in fact is the number one reason why most seek the religion of self-employment. And with no other job opportunities forthcoming the appeal can be driven to a still energetic and talented individual with many "good years" left.

It is true that many of existing small business owners having gone through the same situation are fond of saying; "I wish I would have been fired years ago. It is the best thing that has happened to me." That is wonderful, they have worked hard, perhaps in a related field of their previous employment and experience, and they are reaping the fruits of their labor and efforts, but they are in the minority as far more have gone the other way. It is at this most vulnerable time that a business plan will truly serve well. At this stage it is extremely important to exercise personal introspection in learning what are the actual characteristics and expectation of the entrepreneur. If many years were spend in the shelter of the corporate womb, there is much that was taken for granted that will not be available to the fledgling business and to strain a new business to supply them may be the very straw that will doom it; perks like benefits, comfortable compensation, staff, office and infrastructure, expense account, company automobile, paid travel, etc. all will have to be supplied by the business which may very well not be able to afford it. The entrepreneur may be in for a culture shock as for some time he/she may be wearing all the hats of salesperson, bookkeeper, net-worker, promoter, delivery person, and janitor. For all these reasons the personal characteristics and business expectations are of vital importance and may be found by preparing a business plan. The enterpriser should first strive on paper to determine the ventures feasibility and fit before investing life savings or home equity into a business that they do not care for or one that cannot deliver the comfort level and security that a job had for many years.

This introspective communication is essential with the realization that the first audience for the business plan is the entrepreneur.

The personal criteria of job security, money, lifestyle, insurance, personal health conditions, age, and family considerations are all factors equally as important as product, market, and cash flow management to be considered before an older person of many "good years" who perhaps is not familiar with the guerilla warfare of entrepreneurship should consider and explore with a business plan before starting a business. Their very years of work experience, be it ten or twenty which is often in an isolated world one year's experience twenty times, arms them with a cavalier attitude of someone with my experience can handle this, let's do it. This is not to advocate not to explore a new venture, but to simply encourage that it is done right. Personal question to be answer are as follows:

- Will the business generate sufficient money to meet business expenses and the business owner's personal minimum needs of salary, benefits, and profits?
- What does your spouse and family think of this venture and do you have their support?

- How much debt will the business need, can it be raised and services, and what is your tolerance for debt, how debt adverse are you?
- Are you willing to give up some ownership, control, for equity investment?
- What are the legal requirements and regulations, if any, for the business and its location?

For these and other questions a wise entrepreneur will want to prepare first and foremost a Business Plan to determine if the venture is feasible for him and him for it.

Having established the feasibility of the business concept from the viewpoint of personal planning; now, the Business Plan will take on a new audience and should be rewritten accordingly for the different purpose.

The entrepreneur has proven to himself the feasibility and potential of the business, now, he must pragmatically prove it to others and sell the concept to investors, lenders, key employees, vendors, and perhaps family and friends. The Business Plan now will perform the function as detailed in appendix A-1 and should strive to answer all applicable question outlined in appendix A-2. It is now a true planning tool in which the business model can be refined.

Prior to presentation to interested parties, the business owner can think and make mistakes on paper rather than in the business avoiding wasting real money, resources, and time. Once the business is operational the Business Plan will prove itself truly as a dynamic management tool to evaluate, manage, and monitor operations, sales, profit goals, and the all-important cash flow. As the business progresses and actual performance is compared to projected performance and deviations are analysis, the plan can be rewritten to adjust tactics, activity, and goals to reflect new realities. Such monitoring and financial management by percentages and ratio-analysis against projection, history if any, or benchmark companies initiating adjustments to the plans goals and projections which have now become the planning budget, can be called "rolling revisions" and is most effective if done quarterly. Any time sooner would not have indicated a true trend or a conscientious persistent effort to implement the originally conceived well thought-out plan; any time longer, semi-annually or annually, will have been too long to effectively initiate corrective action.

THE BUSINESS PLAN

A Business Plan truly serves three vital functions:

1. It is a tool for the entrepreneur to develop the idea and concept and determine if it is right for him.

2. It is a retrospective planning tool to compare actual performance to projected performance and goals to implement corrective action if necessary, and

3. It is essential in raising money, both debt and equity. Most investors and lenders will not put capital into a business without seeing a Business Plan that shows that the business concept is well thought out, has a good product and a reachable target market, good cost and profit structure, and most importantly has a good management team.

In the role of presentation to investors and lenders to raise capital, the Business Plan becomes a sales tool. As such the written plan, and if fortunate enough to make a visual and oral presentation (appendix A-1a) must be factual and not wildly exaggerated and yet convey a sense of positive conservative optimism and excitement. If there are any negative risk or adverse competitive issues, they should be acknowledged but not with undue emphasis. The Business Plan should be written objectively realizing again that in the role of raising money, the first role of the Business Plan is to the entrepreneur and it is better for him not to get funding for a bad risk and if the plan so shows that it is not a good venture then it has done its job.

In the role of raising money, the Business Plan should (as detailed in appendix A-1) be as concise and clear as possible explaining how much money is required, for what purpose and what it will do for the business, and how will it be paid back and when. It should sufficiently answer all the question about the company, the industry, the product, the market and marketing, the facility, give the financials (historical and projected), and most importantly the management team, their skills, knowledge, and experience and even their vision of where the company is going – be sure that it is consistent.

As with any business communication, the communicator, whether in writing or verbal, must know the audience. Most business plans are prepared from the entrepreneur's viewpoint; in the selling role it must be from the viewpoint of the lender or investor.

> *"If everyone is thinking alike, then somebody isn't thinking."*
> Gen. George Patton

This role for the Business Plan as a selling tool in raising capital is only the beginning of the documentation to be requested by lenders and investors.

A well thought out and researched Business Plan will help the entrepreneur walk through the business concept on paper first before committing resources and time, bring some objectivity to an idea which may be ill-conceived avoiding the negatives and limitations which may be present. It will help avoid the "beautiful baby syndrome" of since it is my baby it must be the most beautiful baby in the world; when someone else, like a lender, looking at the baby objectively may not consider it so beautiful. A realistically prepared Business Plan should help to avoid an enthusiastic rush into an undercapitalized business which will create disastrous negative cash flow.

The Plan should reflect upon essential details of financing (type and from where), competition (who and how formidable), market (target, size, and how to capture), management (ability and experience of past success), strengths and weakness (organizational and personal), an entire strategic plan.

A Business Plan should reveal that the planner is aware of the **"Six P's of Business – Proper prior planning prevents poor performance."**

The prudent entrepreneur in his zeal to sell the business to a capital provider must be careful not to sell himself on a business that is not feasible.

In business planning the entrepreneur is often alone, particularly in a start-up venture, without the resources for sophisticated financial help, and even with, the ultimate decision is always his/hers. "In the final analysis, we are all alone."

The concept of complete control over the operations of the business is a demanding responsibility and the entrepreneur will wear all the hats of management, making decisions often alone. Therefore, the entrepreneur must be aware of all facets of the business and must understand what the financial numbers mean.

The necessities of meeting payroll, buying inventory and equipment, extending receivables, marketing, paying expenses, and implementing plans to achieve objectives and goals require skills and financial resources often when such are scarce.

Financial planning and management is more than the all-important task of raising the needed cash. Beyond obtaining cash, the decision as how to apply, conserve, and generate more funds are diverse and all involve money or credit. Financial planning is about managing money and credit and about the analysis of and planning for the financial effects of all decisions.

- Evaluating financial performance and position and adjusting the plan when necessary to achieve objectives
- Planning for the future and present needs to achieve future goals
- Managing the assets and liabilities essential for sustained business and profitably growth.

Required is a working knowledge of:

- Basic financial statements
- Cash flow, sources and uses of cash
- Financial Ratio analysis
- Break Even analysis
- Profit planning and pro-forma statements
- Cash, working capital, accounts receivable and payables management
- Inventory management

The financials in a Business Plan are of vital importance. After all it is the numbers which are the language of the business. In a Start-up, the pro-forma, projected statements make for interesting reading but are only that-projection of what might be. They must be sold as feasible in the effort toward sustainable profits and investor's returns.

In an existing business striving for additional capital to expand and further increase the potential of enhancing profitability and building value, the financials tell the past story which an indication of the capacity are should be to build upon for further success.

To communicate these possibilities an understanding and familiarity of the financials, the language of the business, is necessary.

As such the following will be helpful:

ACCOUNTING REVISITED

> *"Not everything that can be counted counts and not everything that counts can be counted."*
> Albert Einstein

FINANCIAL STATEMENTS

The Balance Sheet

The balance sheet is a snapshot of the financial condition, what a business owns and owes at a given moment in time. Its main intention is to provide all interested parties, owners, managers, bankers, and suppliers, a listing and as accurate as possible estimation of the value of all assets and liabilities with the resulting owner's equity position.

The balance sheet accounting equation is:

ASSETS = LIABILITIES + OWNER'S EQUITY,

OR

ASSETS − LIABILITIES = OWNER'S EQUITY,

OR

OWNER'S EQUITY = ASSETS - LIABILITIES

The equation is an algebraic relationship, the equality of which must be maintained;

i.e. whatever is done to the left side of the equation, the opposite must be done to the left side of the equation or do the same to the right side of the equation.

THE BUSINESS PLAN

The two-sided nature of the accounting equation is the basis for double entry accounting that records both sides of the company's transaction – what is received and what is given in the economic exchange.

Assets are the economic resources owned by the business (cash, accounts receivable, inventory, equipment, and buildings) that are expected to benefit future time periods.

Cash and cash equivalents, such as short-term investments maturing in less than one year, are the most liquid and enable a company to meet current obligations.

Accounts Receivable is too often a large portion of current assets. Most companies either compelled by industry and market demands must sell on credit. As such they allow their customers to pay later which may not always be timely to meet current obligations. As a result, accounts receivable must be monitored carefully to assure the company's liquidity. Unfortunately, resulting from poor credit judgment in allowing the purchase on time or general economic conditions, doubtful accounts can arise when the debtor will not pay the obligation greatly impairing the company's ability to meet its obligations.

Inventory is another major portion of current assets. It is easy for a company to become lackadaisical about inventory quantities. Often too large a level of inventory will accumulate because of bulk or bargain buyer with the thought of saving money. If rapid sales do not materialize, such purchases will result in a wasteful tie-up of essential working capital which will cost more than any purchase savings. Besides the drain on cash, there is the need to care for and protect the inventory, additional space, insurance, and the ever-present danger of damage, pilfering and fire. Accounting for inventory won't help this drain rather using LIFO (last-in, first-out) method, or FIFO (first-in, first-out) method. Regretfully, with inattention to inventory levels and purchasing, the method will be FISH (first-in, still here).

Liabilities are the economic obligations of a business (debts owed to banks, finance companies, individuals, suppliers and other accounts payable) to be paid at a definite time in return for a past or current benefit.

Owner's Equity may also be called net worth or shareholder's equity is the owners' interest in the assets minus the liabilities of the business (the leftovers).

Liabilities and Owner's Equity are the two basic types of claims on a business.

In accordance with generally accepted accounting standards, assets are listed on the debit (left) side of the balance sheet in decreasing order of liquidity. Cash and cash equivalents, the most liquid, is listed first, follow by account receivable (credit sales one step from cash if collectable) and inventory (generally two steps from cash with credit sales); next would be equipment and then the least liquid asset of building and land.

Current assets are those with the expectation to be turned into cash within one year, and noncurrent or fixed assets (also called capital assets) conversion rate into cash is longer than one year. Intangible assets, no liquidity at all) are items such as patents, trademarks, copyrights, licenses, and goodwill.

Liabilities are on the credit (right) side of the balance sheet in increasing order of maturity with the quickest due for payment first. Short-term liabilities are listed first, and long-term liabilities last. Current liabilities are to be paid within one year, and noncurrent liabilities are not due until after one year. Liabilities are followed by Owner's Equity, also on the credit side of the balance sheet, which does not have to be repaid because it is the owner's investment and retained earnings of the company.

Owner's Equity is a residual value. It is equal to whatever is left after deducting all the liabilities from all the assets. If total liabilities exceed total liabilities, the business is technically bankrupt.

The Income Statement

The Income Statement, also called the Profit and Loss (P&L) Statement, presents a summary of the operating and financial activity of revenue and expense that affects changes in the owner's equity. As the Balance Sheet is a snap shot of the company's activity at a given point in time, the Income Statement is a motion picture of how the company has performed for a period of time.

The Income statement equation would be:

Income = Revenues – Expenses

For most businesses net sales are the main source of revenues. Without sales revenue there is no business to monitor and manage. To achieve the contribution margin or gross profit, cost of goods sold or cost of sales (a variable expense which depends on the level of sales) are deducted, sales less cost of goods sold. Therefore, the resulting gross profit is the difference between net sales and the cost of goods sold. To achieve net profit, all fixed operating expense, those cost that are constant regardless of sales activity, e.g. rent, payroll (not commission), utilities, all expense that would be considered overhead, are deducted from gross profit.

The three accounts to monitor carefully are: Net Sales, Cost of Goods Sold, and Operating Expense. They should be measured not simply by dollar amounts but as a percentage of gross sales.

Net sales are the gross sales minus cost of goods sold, allowance for return goods, and discounts.

Cost of goods sold is the cost of sales which includes all direct cost of producing and delivering the product or service including direct labor cost.

Operating expense are all expense including fixed expense and other expense not directly related to producing the product. The general and administrative expense generally referred to as the overhead expense.

The Cash Flow Statement

The Cash Flow Statement is like the Income Statement with the exception that it does not record accrued expenses or revenues but is the recordation of how a company has produced and used from operations, financing, and investing actual cash for a period of time. Cash flow is not the same as accrual basis profits. The bottom line profit in the income statement does not increase cash for the period and is not available to meet current obligations. Cash flow almost always differs from the amount of bottom line profit reported in the income statement. Positive cash flow is the sustaining lifeblood of the business. No matter how much cash you have flowing in, it never seems enough to cover what is flowing out.

Operating activities include net income or loss, depreciation, and changes in current assets and current liabilities.

Investing activities are the purchase, sale, or investment in fixed assets, such as real estate, buildings, and equipment.

Financing activities is the cash raised by borrowing money or selling stocks or bonds, and the cash used to pay loans, dividends, or buy back stock and redeem bonds.

A Break-Even analysis would assist a company in managing cost and revenue to cover variable and fixed expenses to plan for profit goals. The break-even analysis is described in the Business Plan appendix (A-1).

The three financial statements, the balance sheet, the income statement, and the cash flow statement may appear to be separate and stand alone, but in fact they are intertwined and interconnected and fit together like pieces of a puzzle; the puzzle that is your business.

To assist in solving the puzzle, the key financial ratios in the glossary will provide a picture of the financial activity affecting your business.

BALANCE SHEETS

A Balance Sheet is a **snapshot** of a business financial condition at a **specific moment in time,** usually at the close of an accounting period. A balance sheet comprises assets, liabilities, and owners' or stockholders' equity. Assets and liabilities are divided into short-term and long-term including cash accounts such as checking, money market, or government securities. At any given time, assets must equal liabilities plus owners' equity (recall the accounting equation A=L+OE). An asset is anything the business owns that has a monetary value. Liabilities are the claims of creditors against the assets of the business.

What is a Balance Sheet used for?

A balance sheet helps a small business owner quickly get a handle on the financial strength and capabilities of the business. Is the business in a position to expand? Can the business easily handle the normal financial ebbs and flows of revenues and expenses? Or should the business take immediate steps to raise cash reserves?

THE BUSINESS PLAN

Balance sheets can identify and analyze trends, particularly in receivables and payables. Is the receivables cycle lengthening? Can receivables be collected more aggressively? Are some receivables uncollectable? Has the business been slowing down payables to forestall an inevitable cash shortage?

Balance sheets, along with income statements, are the most basic elements in providing financial reporting to lenders such as banks, commercial finance companies, investors, and vendors who are considering how much credit to grant the business.

ASSETS

Assets are subdivided into current and long-term assets to reflect the ease of liquidating each asset. Cash, for obvious reasons, is considered the most liquid of all assets. Long-term assets, such as real estate or machinery, are less likely to sell overnight or have the capability of being quickly converted into a current asset such as cash.

CURRENT ASSETS

Current assets are any asset that can be easily converted into cash within one calendar year. Examples of current assets would be checking or money market accounts, accounts receivable, and notes receivable that are due within one year's time.

CASH

Money available immediately, such as in checking accounts, is the most liquid of all short-term assets.

ACCOUNTS RECEIVABLE

This is money owed to the business for the purchases made by the customers.

INVENTORY

Consists of products that are ready for sale; There is an also Material product to be used in production and Work in Process inventory on which production has been started but not yet finished.

NOTES RECEIVABLES

Notes receivables that are due within one year are current assets. Notes that cannot be collected within one year should be considered long-term assets.

FIXED ASSETS

Fixed assets include land, building, machinery, and vehicles that are used in connection with the business.

LAND

Land is considered a fixed asset but, unlike other fixed assets, is not depreciated, because land is considered an asset that never wears out.

BUILDINGS

Buildings are categorized as fixed assets and are depreciated over time.

OFFICE EQUIPMENT

This includes office equipment such as copiers, fax machines, printers, and computers used in your business.

MACHINERY

This represents machines and equipment used in your business.

VEHICLES

This would include any vehicles used in your business.

TOTAL FIXED ASSETS

This is the total dollar value of all fixed assets in your business, less any accumulated depreciation.

TOTAL ASSETS

This represents the dollar value of both the short-term and long-term assets of your business.

LIABILITIES and OWNERS' EQUITY

This includes all debts and obligations owned by the business to outside creditors, vendors, or banks, plus the owners' equity.

ACCOUNTS PAYABLE

This is all short-term obligations owed by the business to creditors, suppliers, and other vendors.

NOTES PAYABLE

This represents money owed to banks, mortgage obligations, vehicles loans, and perhaps vendors' loans.

ACCRUED PAYROLL AND WITHHOLDING

This includes any earned wages or withholdings that are owed to or for employees but have not yet been paid.

TOTAL CURRENT LIABILITIES

This is the sum of all current liabilities owed to creditors that must be paid within a one-year time frame.

LONG-TERM LIABILITIES

These are all debts or obligations owed by the business that are due more than one year out from the current date.

OWNERS' EQUITY

Also refer to as stockholders' equity, net worth, or capital. Owners' equity is made up of the initial investment in the business as well as any retained earnings that are reinvested in the business.

RETAINED EARNINGS

These are earnings (profits) reinvested in the business after any deduction for dividends distributed to shareholders as dividend payments.

TOTAL LIABILITIES and OWNERS' EQUITY

This comprises all debts and monies that are owed to outside creditors, vendors, or banks and the remaining monies that are owed to the owners, shareholders, including retained earnings reinvested in the business.

INCOME STATEMENTS

An Income Statement, also known as a profit and loss statement, is a summary of a business' profit or loss during any one given period (**a motion picture**) such as a month, three months, or a year. The income statement records all revenues for a business during the given period, as well as the operating expenses for the business.

WHAT ARE INCOME STATEMENTS USED FOR?

You use an income statement to track revenues and expenses so that you can determine the operating performance of the business over a period. Business owners use these statements to find out what areas of their business are over budget or under budget. Specific items that are causing unexpected expenditures can be pinpointed, such as phone, fax, mail, or supply expenses. Income statements can also track dramatic increases in product returns, cost of goods sold as a percentage of sales. They also are used to determine income tax liability.

It is very important to format an income statement so that it is appropriate to the business being conducted. All businesses will not have the same accounts but will follow GAAP (General Accepted Accounting Principles).

Income statements, along with Balance Sheets, are the most basic elements required by potential lenders, such as banks, investors, and vendors. They will use the financial reporting contained therein to determine credit limits.

1. SALES (REVENUE)

The sales figure represents the amount of revenue generated by the business. The amount recorded here is the total sales, less any product returns or sales discount.

2. COST OF GOODS SOLD

This number represents the cost (variable cost) directly associated with making or acquiring your products. Costs include materials purchased from outside suppliers used in the manufacture of your product, as well as any internal expenses directly expended in the manufacturing process.

GROSS PROFIT

Gross Profit is derived by subtracting the cost of goods sold from net sales. It is also known as the contribution margin. It does not include any operating expenses or income taxes.

3. OPERATING EXPENSES

These are the daily expenses incurred in the operation of the business; including selling, general, and administrative expenses.

SALES SALARIES

These are the salaries plus bonuses and commissions paid to the sales staff.

ADVERTISING

These represents all costs involved in creating and placing multi-media advertising.

OTHER SALES COSTS

These include any cost associated with selling the product. They may include travel, client entertainment, sales meetings, and equipment rental for presentations, copying, or miscellaneous printing costs.

OFFICE SALARIES

These are salaries of full and part-time office personnel.

RENT

The fees incurred to rent or lease office or industrial space.

UTILITIES

The costs for heating, air conditioning, electricity, phone equipment rental, and phone usage.

DEPRECIATION

Depreciation is an annual expense that considers the loss in value of equipment used in the business; a non-cash expense.

OTHER OVERHEAD COSTS

Expense items that do not fall into other categories or cannot be clearly associated with a function are other overhead costs. These may include insurance, office supplies, or cleaning services.

4. TOTAL EXPENSES

This is the total of all expenses incurred in running the business, exclusive of taxes.

5. NET INCOME BEFORE TAXES

This total represents the amount of income earned by the business prior to paying income taxes. This figure is derived by subtracting total operating expenses from gross profit.

6. TAXES

This is the amount of income taxes you owe to the federal government and, if applicable, state and local government taxes.

7. NET INCOME

This is the amount of money the business has earned after paying income taxes.

INCOME AND EXPENSE

On the Balance Sheet, in the beginning of your Accounting System, you had only the three classifications: ASSETS, LIABILITIES, AND CAPITAL.

THE BUSINESS PLAN

One day you sold your cell phone for $100 which you had only paid $50.

So, your cash (asset) goes up $100 and the cell phone account (asset) goes down $50.

But where does the $50 profit go? It isn't an asset (although the increase in cash is an asset, but as an accounting entry how does it get there?) It is not a liability since you don't owe it to anyone. Therefore, it has to go into Equity (to balance the increase in Cash).

> The $50 is called INCOME.
>
> Do you like INCOME? YES! Why; BECAUSE IT INCREASES YOUR EQUITY (WORTH).
>
> The more Income you have, the more you are worth!
>
> Do you like Expenses? NO! BECAUSE THE MORE EXPENSE YOU HAVE, THE LESS YOU ARE WORTH.

Income and Expense are recorded in the Equity (Capital) account.

Income increases Equity... so it increases on the right side of the Equity account.

Expenses decrease Equity... so they increase on the left side of the Equity account.

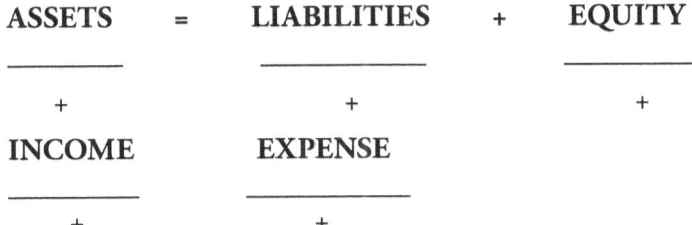

Refer to the Accounting Memo Rules for Debits and Credits.
Remember Debit means Left; and Credit means Right.
If you debit an account, you place the amount on the left side of that account.

If you credit an account, you place the amount on the right side of that account.

The Accounting Equation is an algebraic relationship, the equality of which must be maintained, i.e.

Whatever I do to the left side of the equation, I must do the opposite to the left side of the equation or do the same to the right side of the equation.

Liabilities and Owners' Equity are the two basic types of claims on a company.

The two-sided nature of the accounting equation is the basis for double entry accounting that records both sides of the company's transaction – what is received and what is given in the economic exchange.

RULES FOR DEBITS and CREDITS

Debit means the LEFT side; CREDIT means the RIGHT side

ASSETS are on the left and are debits; Liabilities and Owner's Equity are on the right and are credits.

ASSETS		LIABILITIES and OWNER'S EQUITY	
increase	decrease	decrease	increase
Debits	**Credits**	**Debits**	**Credits**

EXPENSES and LOSSES		REVENUE and INCOME	
increase	decrease	decrease	increase
Debits	**Credits**	**Debits**	**Credits**

Financial Effects of Revenue and Expenses

Revenue = Assets increase (debit) or Liability decrease (debit)
Expense = Asset decrease (credit) or Liability increase (credit)

CHAPTER FOUR

EFFECTIVE PUBLIC SPEAKING

The human mind treats a new idea the way the body treats a strange protein-It rejects it."
Peter Medawar

NOTES ON PUBLIC SPEAKING
"Getting in Front of People"

Every activity of our lives is a communication. Speaking is one way that we assert our distinctiveness from others and from all other forms of life. Business, social, and personal satisfaction depend heavily upon a person's ability to communicate clearly what he /she is, what he/she desires, and what he/she believes in.

When a person is unable to speak clearly due to nerves, timidity, lack of preparation and knowledge, the message will be misunderstood. All social interaction, business and personal, depends upon the ability to communicate clearly. In previous times, speaking was regarded as an art, a performance with grandiose gestures and inflections, it is not. It is a skill which all can learn and master. By having a positive attitude and building on the fundamentals of communication and speaking in a clear, concise manner, all can learn to communicate effectively.

Take heart, no one is born a public speaker. All can learn it. It helps to consider it as an enlarged conversation in which you attempt to convey your thoughts in a very understandable, concise, succinct manner. Be brief. Tell them what you are going to say. Say it. Tell them what you said. The more you go on, the more you will be uninteresting and lose the audience. Always learn about your audience beforehand. If General George Armstrong Custard had, perhaps his last engagement would not have ben a disaster. What do they know about the subject? Are they interested in the subject? What is their level of understanding on the subject? What do they know about you? What benefit is in the subject for them?

The eminent teacher of public speaking, Dale Carnegie, put forth these four rules of the basic skills:

1. Take heart from the experience of others – no one is a natural speaker. Gone is the strict attention to rhetoric and grandiloquent style and stentorian tone. Prepare by analyzing and knowing your audience and simply talk to them in the language and manner that they will understand.

2. Keep your goals before you – to accomplish your objective projected the situation into the future and then work toward bringing it in the present reality.

3. Predetermine your mind to success – your thoughts make you what you are, by changing your thoughts, you change your life. Think positively, not negatively. When Caesar invaded what is now England, he burned his ships before the men informing them that there was no retreat but only to advance and conquer. That is precisely what they did. Make that spirit yours and conquer your fears and convince the audience.

4. Seize every opportunity to practice – To learn to speak in public, you must speak in public. Just like you cannot not learn to swim without getting in the water. To paraphrase George Bernard Shaw to speak convincing do so often by making a fool of yourself until you get used to it.

Management is always looking for those who can communicate effectively and able to win the cooperation of others. A speech is but an extended conversation. Talk with your audience not to them.

Realize that Fear of Public Speaking is universally common. *"Fear defeats more people than any other one thing in the world." Emerson*

Fact Number One – You are not unique to your fear of speaking in public. Eighty to ninety percent suffer from stage fright in my experience it appears to be more like one hundred percent. It, short of dying, is the most common fear we all possess. Often one must be beaten to get in front of people, but once there, often one must be beaten to stop.

Fact Number Two – A certain amount of stage fright is useful. It is nature's way of preparing us to meet the challenge. So, when your heart is pounding, and your respiration is speeding up, don't be alarmed. Your body is getting ready to go into action. Do not announce that you are nervous or frightening. Most of the time the audience will not notice it and any mention would only be distracting.

Fact Number Three – Many professional speakers have stated that they never completely lose all stage fright. It is almost always present just before speaking, and it may persist through the first few sentences.

Fact Number Four – the chief cause of your fear of public speaking is simply that you are unaccustomed to speaking in public. To make this fearful situation simple and easy: prepare and practice, practice, practice. Rehearse your talk with friends and family. Seek the opportunity to speak as often as possible. Only the prepared speaker deserves to be confident. Abraham Lincoln once said, *"I believe that I shall never be old enough to speak without embarrassment when I have nothing to say."*

Preparation does not mean memorizing your talk. Never memorize your talk word for word. It just invites "brain freeze". Instead know your subject, make a few notes, and speak naturally to your audience. All our lives we have been speaking spontaneously. We haven't been thinking of words. We have been thinking of ideas. If our ideas are clear, the words come naturally and unconsciously as the air we breathe.

If you are not anxious about giving a talk or making a presentation you either done it too often or you have no emotions and do not feel strongly about your subject. Do not attempt to suppress this natural nervousness but use it to energize your talk. Your excitement will be contagious and spread to the audience to move them.

A helpful rule of speaking, especially an impromptu talk, is "first tell them what you are going to say; then say it to them; then tell them what you said." Stand up, speak up, shut up. Always strive to use short sentences and be brief with your remarks. However, never talk down to your audience. It will be resented and turn them off.

Act confident. "Feelings follow actions." Don't rush. If you feel that you are going too fast, you are; if you feel like you are going just right, you are still going too fast; if you feel like you are going too slowly, you are going just right.

Prepare more material than is necessary and rehearse before-hand either with others are alone. A surgeon said "I can teach you in ten minutes how to take out an appendix. But it will take me four years to teach you what to do if something goes wrong." Always prepare to be ready for an emergency, such as a question, or changed in emphasis due to a previous speaker's comments.

Think positively and visualize your success. Confidence is projected attitude. An arrogant attitude will not motivated others to perceive the speaker as a winner, someone they want to be with, have faith-in, and trust. Confidence is often broadcasted by body language. Stand erect with good posture. Use straightforward clear positive words filled with enthusiasm and energy. Use appropriate gestures to make emphasis making sure that they are not over-the-top and exaggerated.

Don't let your hands fall below your waist. Use short sentences, simplify everything, and know where the bathroom is.

Do you use visual aids (appendix A-4). Choose which may be most appropriate and helpful for clarity: Overhead transparencies, electronic, chalkboards and whiteboards, flip-charts, and other visual aids. Sometimes, without being too cluttered, the best strategy is to use a combination of aids with hand-outs.

The presenter should always be mindful of the following:
- Tone and quality of voice
- Diction, enunciation, and language
- Breathing, pacing, and phrasing (avoid the "uh,s", "and's", "you know's", etc.
- Nervousness, enthusiasm, and confidence

- General appearance, posture, dress
- Facial expressions, gestures, and eye contact. Make eye-contact, not to just a few, but move your gaze to all. Don't look at the ceiling or the back wall.

TELEPHONE CONVERSATIONS

A much use form of verbal communication we tend to take for granting is the telephone. It is one of the most valuable communication tools at our disposal. Just as you are mindful of appearance of written documents, vocabular of speech, grooming and dress, you should be equally concern with your phone impression, delivery, and etiquette. Your personal telephone image and style is as important as all other forms of communication.

Your phone image is generally a part of three factors, your voice and language, your manners and politeness, and all who answer the phone on your behalf.

NAME RECOGNITION

A person's name is magic. People like being called by name particularly in a sales situation. When you remember a prospects name and use it, they are usually put at ease and feel that you have a special interest in them and their concerns. To assist in remember the name be sure to hear it clearly. Don't hesitate to ask for it again if not received clearly. Better to ask then to mistakenly called someone by the wrong name.

When you use someone's name, the audience becomes part of your talk. You will notice a rise in attention as the audience becomes more aware of themselves and more interested as one of them is brought into attention. This use of audience participation and asking questions will remove the barrier between you and them.

Be mindful that every talk has four basic purposes:

1. To persuade, to get action
2. To inform
3. To impress, convince, motivate, and inspire
4. To entertain.

An additional list about making speeches:

- To communicate, have a clearly defined subject
- An audience understanding is affect by language, style, and organization
- Long words are harder to understand than short words
- Long sentences are harder to understand than short ones
- Do not present many ideas in a short time
- People react better to a speech than what they read
- Appearance, manner, and delivery are important

CHAPTER FIVE

EFFECTIVE WRITTEN COMMUNICATION

"To write well, express yourself like the common people, but think like a wise man."
Aristotle

A written communication is best when it is helpful and important to retain a permanent record of the message and information. It facility your control over the information and helps to reach large groups with minimum confusion and misunderstanding. You, your ideas, and proposals are more often judged by the written than by the spoken words. The written contact often precedes any opportunity for a personal spoken presentation and will be the instrument that set up such an opportunity. Your written submissions will demonstrate your skill and mastery of the subject as well as your ability to express it an organized clear matter.

Some disadvantages of a written format are that it does not provide for immediate feedback and lacks the facial expression and other physical cues of how the message is being received. Also, distribution of the message could be cumbersome and time consuming.

There are three steps in creating an effective written message: Planning, Writing, and Completing.

- Planning. Analyze your audience and the situation. Know how to address them that will assure interest and understanding.

Know what the purpose of the communication and the goals to achieve. Select the best method to communicate, written, electronic e-mail, hard copy letter or memo, and if oral, in-person, group meeting, or via electronic messaging. After determining the audience needs and purpose for the communication, gather and organize information to emphasis and prioritize delivery defining the main idea.

- Writing. Adapt the message to the audience both in words and method of delivery, either direct or indirect. Be positive and uplifting using a conversational tone in plain English not some technical babble. Use strong understandable words in effective sentences as brief and short as possible without talking down to the audience.
- Completing. Rework and revise a first draft to assure readability and understanding. Proofread for the elimination of typos and spelling errors. The message must be concise, succinct with correct grammar, proper punctuation, and a clean format without distracting design or stationary.

It is recommended to best use your writing time, try to use half for planning, one quarter for writing, and one quarter for completing. There is no absolute correct way, but these are general guidelines which help to result in success. Trying to save time on these stages will usually cost you more time.

GOODWILL AND NEGATIVE MESSAGES – written and oral

Goodwill is the positive feeling that people must have to continue in a relationship. An effective goodwill message must be received as sincere, honest, and relative. Otherwise the message will be reflective of your interest and not of the audience.

EXAMPLES

Be respectful, not demanding

        Demanding –   Submit your answer within one week.
        Respectful -   I would appreciate your answer within one week.

Be modest, not arrogant

    Arrogant -   My report is thorough, and I'm sure that you won't find fault with it.
    Modest -   The report is detailed, and I hope you find it satisfactory.

Be polite, not sarcastic

    Sarcastic -   I just now received your test due several weeks ago. I am rejecting it – it is too late. Good luck!
    Polite -   Your test is being returned. Unfortunately, it is too late for grading.

Be positive and tactful, not negative and condescending

    Negative -   Your complaint about our prices is way off target. Our prices are not any higher than those of our competitors.
    Tactful -   Thank you for your suggestion concerning our prices. We believe, however, that they are competitive with, and in some cases are below, those of our competitors.

GOOD NEWS AND BAD NEWS

It is generally more effective to present Good News directly and Bad News indirectly. Often Bad News is best delivered with a buffer providing context, an explanation, the news, and a goodwill positive closing. Although bad news is never pleasant, related information and positive suggestions can put the bad news in perspective or make it seem reasonable and perhaps maintains goodwill between the parties.

Goodwill messages are:

    Congratulations
    Condolence (always be brief)
    Appreciation
    Invitation
    Holiday Greetings
    Welcome

Goodwill messages are delivered by:

    Handwritten – (most popular)
    Typewritten

> Printed
> Card
> Letter
> Informal
> Formal

Delivery of Positive and Neutral messages have four goals:

> To communicate information and good news
> To answer all questions
> To provide all required details
> To leave the recipient with a good impression

OPENING

In the opening, give the positive or neutral information upfront (directly); State the request; be optimistic; provide coherence and relevance; stress receiver interest and benefits.

EXPLANATION

Present related information; explain and justify the request; be objective; be concise; be positive.

SALES APPEAL (if appropriate)

Personalize appeal; suggest alternative if appropriate; aim for quick action and closing.

FRIENDLY CLOSE

Build goodwill; reasons for action; be concise; be positive; provide contact information; express appreciation.

NEGATIVE MESSAGES

NO is hard to say and hard to hear. Unfortunately, negative messages are sometimes required. In doing so there are usually four objectives: to convey bad news, to gain its acceptance, to salvage as much goodwill as possible, and to avoid the need for further communication on the matter.

THE OPENING BUFFER

    Provide coherence
    Build goodwill
    Be positive
    Maintain neutrality
    Explanation

THE EXPLANATION

    Relate to the opening buffer
    Present convincing reasoning
    Stress receiver's interest and benefits
    Be positive

THE NEGATIVE INFORMATION

    Relate to the explanation
    Give negative information explicitly
    Give negative information quickly
    Be positive
    Say what can be done (not what cannot)
    Avoid an apology

THE CONSTRUCTIVE FOLLOW-UP

    Provide alternative solution

THE FRIENDLY CLOSE

    Build goodwill
    Personalize the close
    Stay off the negative subject
    Be warm
    Be optimistic

There are five goals in conveying Negative News:

    To convey the bad news
    To gain acceptance for it
    To maintain as much goodwill as possible
    To maintain a good image for the organization
    To eliminate/reduce the need for future discussion/correspondence on the matter

Some phases to avoid when conveying negative news:

"I'm afraid that we cannot" ….

> Not afraid, hiding behind an empty phrase

"I'm sorry that we are unable" …

> Not sorry, probably are able – If so sorry about saying NO, why not change policy and say YES

"I'm sure you will agree that" …

> Don't assume that you can read their mind

"Unfortunately," …

> Is negative and signals that a refusal is coming

"Will take under consideration" …

> Always signals a NO is coming

Credibility

The audience will be more receptive of your message if they have confidence in you. Their perception of your credibility is their belief in your reliability, truthfulness, intentions, and trust. With existing associates, vendors, investors, creditors, employees, and customer, you have already established a relationship which hopefully is favorable based on past experiences. However, with a new audience, that relationship is yet to be established if your message will be well received and invokes the desired result.

The following factors will assist in that effort:

- Honesty. Credibility is built on honesty. If you don't tell the truth, people will not believe in you nor act favorably toward your message. If successful in establishing integrity by demonstrating honesty you will earn the trust of the audience even if they perhaps do not agree with you.
- Objectivity. People always appreciate the sender's ability to disassociate from emotions and present the issue from all viewpoints and sides. They will believe that you are not only interested in your opinion but also theirs.
- Audience awareness. They must know that you understand what is important to them and that you know what you are talking about. By putting yourself in their position establish

your credentials and knowledge in a humble unarrogant way without disrupting the message. Often an endorsement from someone they trust will be helpful in establishing your acceptance.

Your written image should be readable, understandable, interesting, persuasive, positive, and personal. To appeal personality to an individual, use the person's name.

Be mindful that while arrogance will turn people off, too little confidence or too much modesty can hurt your acceptance and credibility.

Always use plain English in a conversational but businesslike manner. Avoid obsolete and pompous words as well as any bragging about accomplishments or preaching giving the impression that you know more than them. Use short sentences. Keep them simple. "KISS" keep it simple and short. Be direct and write in the present tense.

LETTERS

Like meetings formal letter writing, while declining in use, will always be a necessity in conducting and concluding business. Letters are most use to individuals outside of the organization or within when a formal written record is desired. As such the appearance is important as all other forms of communication if it is to be received well. It may very well be the first introductory impression that the reader is receiving. And, first impressions are very important especially in soliciting investment, information, cooperation, and sales. Its contents must be clearly understood in as concise and succinct manner as possible. The appearance of a formal letter should be in accordance as the standard acceptable format. Such as the uniform parts of the letter, punctuation, style, grammar, and stationary.

As a reminder, a formal letter contains seven parts: Heading, inside address, salutation, body, complimentary close, and signature.

It is often helpful to also have an attention line as part of the inside address, and a subject line identifying the main subject of the letter.

If lacking in formal letter structure, it would be helpful to have a business correspondence handbook available.

$ENTREPRENEUR COMMUNICATION$

The envelope should be of the same color and quality as the stationery and, of course, should be of appropriate size to hold the letter and any enclosures. In addition to the mailing address, the envelope should contain a return address.

CHAPTER SIX

RESUMES

"The greater danger for most of us lies not in setting our aim too high and falling short; but in setting our aim too low and achieving our mark."
Michelangelo

Few documents and presentations are more important to the entrepreneur and individual as the business plan and the resume. Both are vital to any business and career endeavor and are complemental to each other. A well-prepared resume belongs in a well-prepared business plan as it reveals and sells the individual who will make the business model work to investors, creditors, vendors, and potential employees. It is equally important when seeking a personal employment opportunity for, much like a business plan, it will open the door for further discussion.

In both, appearance is paramount and should not be quickly and sloppy prepared. They are representative of you, an introduction into your abilities and potential. Both should amply illustrate how you will contribute to the overall mission of the venture or of the organization to which you are applying.

The appearance will have a great impression on the reader. The paper, font, design, and format all play a role. Attention to detail such as spelling, grammar, and word choice are all important. This initial impression will determine if a follow-up visit will be forthcoming. Reverse chronological order of work experience is generally preferred.

TEN RULES FOR A SUCCESSFUL RESUME

1. **BE BRIEF:**

    If an employer is actively searching for a new person, chances are he or she will receive many resumes. The employer must read through most or all of them. The key to keeping the employer's interest is to make sure every word counts for something in your document and to keep it as short as possible. When possible, keep it to one page. The employer is only going to have a few minutes to review the resume, so make sure it is time well spent. KISS; keep it simple and short, concise and succinct. If essential, you may expound in the cover letter.

2. **BE SUBSTANTIVE:**

    Potential employers are reading your resume only to see what you have done professionally. Any other information can be communicated in a cover letter, or face-to-face in a job interview. Focus your resume writing on what really counts.

3. **PRIORITIZE:**

    You may have a lot to say about each job you have had, but some of it will not fit into your resume. Employers do not need to know that you were named employee of the month 10 years ago, or that you organized the office Christmas party. The former happened long ago, and the latter likely has little to do with your abilities as an employee. Determine what elements of your occupational history add up to make you a truly marketable person, a contributor, and a good hire.

4. **BE PERTINENT:**

    It is important to keep your material focused only on those elements that would directly relate to your hirability. If an employer can see that you have steadily progressed in your career; achieved certain benchmarks and accomplished things that furthered your previous employer's mission, that may go a long way toward landing the new job. <u>Employers do not need to know your hobbies, your family life or your opinions on issues not related to the job.</u>

5. **BE SELECTIVE:**

It is up to you how much information you reveal in your resume. Generally, it is not advisable, for example, to offer your specific salary history. This can work against you; first, the employer may feel you are too expensive. Further, you may undercut your opportunity to increase your salary if your previous earnings appear too low. Think carefully about what you want the potential employer to know about you.

6. **BE ACCESSIBLE:**

If possible, offer multiple methods to contact you. These might include your home phone number, cell phone number, email address, and mailing address. During your job search check your messages frequently and return calls the same day they are received.

7. **EMPHASIZE RELEVANT EXPERIENCE:**

If you are applying for a job as a sales account executive, for example, employers need to see what you have done that would directly relate to the job. However, if you have held other job types that require skills common to sales, you should mention them and briefly explain the relevant skills or experience.

8. **REFERENCES DO NOT NECESSARILY HAVE TO BE INCLUDED IN YOUR RESUME:**

You may want to use the space you have to further describe your credentials. However, when you go to your job interview, have a list of your references available.

9. **PRESENTATION COUNTS:**

Your resume should be printed on good white paper. Use a readable font, at least 10 points, preferably 12, and be sure your printer is producing good readable copy.

10. **PROOFREAD YOUR RESUME MULTIPLE TIMES AND, IF POSSIBLE, HAVE ANOTHER PERSON PROOFREAD IT.**

Make sure grammar, spelling, and word choice are all accurate. The resume is a representation of you, and possibly the first impression an employer will have of you. It must be perfected worded, structured and presented.

COVER LETTER

A well written concise cover letter will help introduce your resume. The reader and potential employer will too often invest a very limited time in viewing the resume. An inviting cover letter is a brief first impression and will enhance the readers interest to read further. They will also help to personalize the application process prior to a potential visit. It should briefly outline specific skills that your research has indicated would be of interest to the organization. It should never be generically address but to an individual in the organization. It should be as well written as any other professional document with attention to appearance, grammar, spelling, and format. List only your very best skills that relate to the position you are applying, and always request a follow-up meeting.

Make sure it is not longer than one page and is printed on the same stationary as your resume and that it is signed.

TEN WAYS TO GET YOUR RESUME IGNORED

1. **Not bothering with a cover letter:**

Many hiring managers automatically reject resumes that arrive without a cover letter. Make the most of your cover letter by expanding on a few of your qualifications, explaining any gaps in employment or providing other information that will entice the employer to read your resume.

2. **Giving your resume format a little flair:**

Unusual fonts, too small fonts, or fluorescent pink paper will certainly make your resume stand out – **in a bad way.** Keep your resume looking professional by sticking with standard white paper, black type and a common font like Arial or Times New Roman.

3. **Going long:**

Your high school job scooping ice cream probably isn't relevant to your career anymore, so there is no reason to include it on your resume. Your resume should be no longer than two pages—and no more than a page for most professionals—so only include your most recent and relevant work history.

4. **Focus on duties, not accomplishments:**

Instead of writing a list of job duties on your resume, demonstrate how each duty contributed to your company's bottom line.

5. **Having a selfish objective:**

employers are trying to determine whether you are a good fit for their organizations, so everything on your resume should point to your experience. A summary of qualifications that conveniently displays your accomplishments is far more effective than a generic objective statement.

6. **Being too generic:**

Always customize your resume and cover letter for each job and employer to which you apply. No "to whom it may concern." Customize to tailor your material to show how you will be a perfect fit for the position.

7. **Guesstimating your dates and titles:**

With background checks, any upgrades you give your titles or stretching of employment dates to cover gaps will likely get caught – and you will be eliminated from consideration.

8. **Tell everyone why you left:**

Never put anything negative on your resume. If you left a position due to a layoff or you were fired, bring it up only if asked.

9. **Include lots of personal information:**

It doesn't belong on your professional resume. This includes your height, weight, religious affiliation, sexual orientation or any other facts that could potentially be used against you.

10. **Assume spell-check is good enough:**

Spell-check can pick up many, typos-but it won't catch everything (manger vs. manager). Always proofread your resume several times and ask a friend to do so.

TEN THINGS THAT WILL GET YOU HIRED

1. **Customize your resume and cover letter:**

It might seem faster to blast off generic materials to dozens of employers, but this will cost you time in the long run. Tailor your resume and cover letter to each open position to clearly demonstrate how your experience fills the employers' requirements.

2. **Diversify your search:**

If you have been responding to newspaper ads with no response, also post your resume online, search some job web sites, talk to your friends and attend an industry trade show. The more ways you search, the more likely you are to connect with the right employers.

3. **Don't go solo:**

Your friends, family, former co-workers, and teachers each have a network of their own – and a friend-of-a-friend might hold the perfect lead. Don't be shy; Reach out to your network and let your contacts know you are on the job market.

4. **Find a company where you fit in:**

Browse potential employers 'web sites and ask your friends about what it's like to work at their companies. Employers are looking for candidates who would be a good fit and thrive within the company culture.

5. **Don't get discouraged:**

Experts estimate the average job search to last anywhere between three and 12 months – and that means a lot of rejection. Keep at it; be persistent. "It's always too soon to give up!"

6. **Always be prepared:**

You can never be too prepared for your first meeting with potential employers. Before your interview, always browse the company's web site. Find out as much as you can about the company's products, leadership, mission and culture, and prepare answers to common interview questions.

7. **Be on time:**

Whether it's an information interview, open houses, or a formal interview, always arrive about ten minutes early. Allow plenty of time for traffic and poor weather. It shows interest and good planning.

8. **Dress and act the part:**

In a business setting, always dress in professional clothing in the best quality you can afford. Take the industry and employer into consideration, but a business suit is almost always appropriate for interviews.

9. **Listen more than you talk:**

Even if you are nervous at an interview, try not to ramble. By keeping your mouth shut, you can learn valuable information and avoid saying something that you will wish you hadn't. And you may learn what is of special interest to address.

10. **Ask good questions:**

At the end of an interview, the employer will inevitably ask if you have any questions. Have a list of questions prepared, preferably in mind not on paper, that showcase your company research and interest in the position.

INTERVIEW

The well-prepared resume and cover letter will hopefully result in the interview. This is your opportunity to impress. All the excruciate appearance details attending to in preparation of your written documents are increasing important in the personal meeting.

Dress is important and should be appropriate for the situation. Clothing, of course, should be clean and in a conservative color with minimum jewelry. Personal hygiene should be immaculate, hair, nails, beard, either clean-shaven or (if appropriate) well-trimmed and like those worn by most existing employees.

If you are being interviewed, in your preparation, ask yourself these questions:

- What is my purpose and goal for this interview? How does it fit the purpose of the interviewer?

- Have I gather sufficient information about the organization? What do you know about the interviewer?
- Have all possible short-comings and slip-ups been anticipated and eliminated?
- Have I prepared for anticipated and expected questions? Do I have any necessary documents?
- Is my appearance and dress appropriate?

Prepare for the interview questions by doing your company research and be aware of the organization mission, business-model, products/service, and market. Remember that the primary reason for the interview is to determine if you have the skills, experience, altitude to contribute and fit in with the rest of the team and company culture. Expect to answer questions and be prepared to ask your own.

TEN TYPICAL QUESTIONS FROM THE INTERVIEW

1. **Why did you leave your last job?**

You are trying to further your career and take the next logical occupational step. If, however, you left because you hated your job or your boss, this is not the time or place to mention that. Stay positive and demonstrate a progressive, mature attitude.

2. **Why do you want to work for us?**

You should have done some research into the company, its products or services, and the responsibilities associated with the job. Show that you know something about the company and the position, and honestly say why you would like to work there.

3. **Why should we hire you for this position?**

Let the interviewer know what you are capable of and what you bring to the company that will contribute to the overall mission.

4. **What are your strengths?**

Keep your response centered on your professional strengths and those aspects of your character that will positively add something to the company. Remember they want someone who is diligent, hardworking, and who can work well independently yet still function effectively as a member of the team.

5. **What are your weaknesses?**

This is tricky territory. If you lack a certain area of training, or certification for a specific job type, you should be honest about that. If they sense that you are determining to improve and enhance your qualifications and are in the process of doing so, chances are you may still be considered.

6. **Where do you see yourself in five years?**

Employers want to know if they can count on you for the long term since they will be spending resources on your training for the job. Try to establish yourself as a reliable person seeking occupational stability and one who may be a long-term employee.

7. **How do you work under pressure?**

Most jobs have some stressful moments, and they are trying to find out how you will handle it. It is important to be able to approach a job one element at a time and not be overwhelmed by a stressful bigger picture. Demonstrate that you are organized, responsible and that you are not one to panic in a pressure situation and let it affect your job performance.

8. **Do you have any questions for me?**

The answer should always be "YES." If you have done your homework there will be things you want to know about the company's growth and development, expansion plans and what your place might be in those plans. Remember, it is not good form to ask about salary in this first meeting. Ask about broader issues, such as possible advancement over time, work environment and specific responsibilities.

9. **Are you applying for other positions?**

Do not hesitate to let them know that you are in the middle of a full job search, and that you have applied for other jobs. This may work in your favor, especially if they are impressed with your experience and your performance in the interview.

10. **Tell me a little about yourself.**

The employer wants to know what type of individual you are. Keep your response focused on aspects of your life and character that would directly and positively affect your job performance. If you are someone who never gives up until the job is done, say it. If you are someone that has always demonstrated natural leadership qualities, say it. If you have always been a good team player, say it. Tell them things about yourself that will give them a good reason to hire you.

You should also be prepared to ask the following:

1. Why is this position vacant? And, how long has it been opened?
2. What does success in this position look like in the first 90 days?
3. What challenges will I face in the first 90 days?
4. What challenges is the company currently facing and how are they being addressed?
5. How do you retain your top talent who contributes to the company's mission?
6. Why do you work for this company and what has been your experience?

Within two to three days a follow-up thank-you letter would be advantageous. Most do not send one, therefore this will make your application stand out and afford you to briefly express your desire to join the organization and enumerate how your skills will contribute to its success.

CHAPTER SEVEN

GRAMMAR REVISTED

"Everything bows to success, even grammar."
Victor Hugo

There has been much discussion about appearance in personal, dress, written, and oral.

Nothing is more negative and will stand out as a poorly prepared and sloppy documents or speech in which inadequate grammar and poor vocabulary is used. Communication goals will not be achieved and in fact the audience will be turned off and lost.

The mechanics of good grammar are simply the way that words are contained in sentences and paragraphs. It is how words come together to form ideas in sentences.

Ideas that will inform and inspire and to do so they must be structured to be clearly understood. Once there is understanding the intended action will be easy. Business readers are different from leisure readers in that they want efficiency and clarity in the very first read.

Remember the readers are more interested in how the message relates to them than how it affects you.

A Brief Refresher

Words can be classified as parts of speech according to what they mean outside of the sentence but mostly by how they are used in a sentence. A sentence is a group of words expressing a statement, question, or command.

Nine parts of speech:

NOUN -	Person, Place, or Thing
PRONOUN -	Word used in place of a noun – *he, she*
VERB -	Action word – He *runs* fast.
ADJECTIVE -	Modifies a noun or pronoun – The *ugly* runs fast.
ADVERB -	Modifies a verb, an adjective, or another adverb – The *fat* ugly duck runs *very* fast.
PREPOSITION -	Word that has a noun or pronoun as its object and forms with that object one modifying unit called a phase - The fat ugly duck *in* the yard runs fast.
CONJUNCTION -	Word or group of words whose purpose is to connect sentence parts, sentences, and paragraphs. It does not take an object. The fat ugly duck *and* the skinny pig are both fast runners.
EXCLAMATORY WORD -	Word or group of words that express emotion but has no grammatical connection with the rest of the sentence. *Oh!* The ugly fat duck is dead.
DUMMY SUBJECT -	Is the word *it* or *there* used simply to indicate that the subject is coming after the predicate verb or to avoid awkward construction. *It* was plain the duck was sick. *There* were no duck doctors.

THREE VERBALS: GERUND, PARTICIPLE, INFINITIVE

GERUND –   A verb-noun ending in *ing*, names an action –
               The duck's *running* is all over.
PARTICIPLE -   A verb-adjective –
               The *dying* duck ran no more.
INFINITIVE -   A verb-noun, introduced by *to*, it names an action.
               It is too late for the duck *to run*.

Examples of some words misuse and expressions:

He went too the store two buy to apples.
s/b:
He went to the store to buy two apples.

To – preposition
Too – adverb
Two – adjective

I don't want none.
DOUBLE NEGATIVE
s/b:
I don't want any.

He plays football good.
s/b:
He plays football well.

Good – pronoun
Well – adverb

You are good.
You do well.

Foot and feet
It is one foot, but anything above one is feet; i.e. five feet not five foot.

Affect means to influence
Effect means to accomplish

Bring and Take: you bring things here; you take them there.

Farther and further: Farther is a physical distance, Further is a figurative distance.
New Orleans is "farther" than Baton Rouge. The Business plan can go no "Further".

"Mise" is not an acceptable abbreviation for "might as well".

Er and est :
Something is great; if two then one is greater than the other; if three or more then one is the greatest of them all.

Hyphen when the words go together as one:
Last-ditch, Mother-in-law.

I.E. stands for the Latin Id est, "that is"
E.G. stands for the Latin exempli gratia, "for example"

When using numbers –
1-9 use verbal, one, two, etc.
Above nine use the numerical, 10, 11, 12, etc. except when beginning a sentence then use the verbal.

Spelling rules:

I before E, except after C – or when sounded as A, as in neighing and weigh.

When verbs end in "ie", change the ending to "y" before adding "ing".
i.e. die, dying, lie, lying, tie, tying

PUNCTUATION:

Period – Put a period at the end of a declarative sentence or indirect question.

>Rain is wet. I wonder what's wrong.

Comma – use a comma to separate words and phrases in a series.

    He's ready to go, wait for me.

Semicolon – use between clauses in a compound sentence when the conjunction is omitted or when the connection is closed.

    The statistical evidence is there; it cannot be denied.

Colon – use to begin a list.

    He studied three subjects: Biology, Chemistry, and English.

Quotation Marks – use around a direct quote

    He said, "Go away." (period always goes in the quotation marks.)

Apostrophe – use for contractions

    "It's" all right. (for it is)

Question Mark – use for questions.

    What on earth do you mean?

Exclamation Mark – use to express strong feelings.

    That's crazy!

It is advisable to have a grammar handbook handy when ever composing a business document. Especially if it is a formal request or sales presentation. Never have your proposal or vision reject or misunderstood due to an ill prepared document that would nor project the image desired or convey the information intended.

CHAPTER EIGHT

INTERCULTURAL COMMUNICATION

> *"Alice said, would you please tell me which way to go from here? The cat said, "that depends on where you want to get to."*
> Lewis Carroll

Recall that there is no communication without understanding. One of the obstacles to assuring that the idea, concept, information is received is the lack of comprehension. Consequently, there will be no movement to action or resolution, no motivation, and no inspiration toward a team effort.

Intercultural communication is the sending and receiving of messages between those whose culture could cause them to misunderstand the messages. Every message received or send is influenced by the cultural background of the sender and/or receiver. Therefore, as part of knowing your audience either as a sender or a receiver, you must be aware of and grasp these differences in understanding to communicate successful. Accomplishing this bridge to understanding and overcoming this obstacle will greatly enhance the ability to understand and communicate successful. Additionally, there is the potential to maximize the efforts of a diverse workforce and sales representatives for expanded business opportunities.

In this global marketplace, the need to communicate with individuals from different cultures and backgrounds is ever increasing. At some time in your entrepreneurial endeavors it will be advantageous to do business and seek opportunities across borders. An awareness of the cultural differences and a familiarity with the language will make these opportunities a reality. Due to the advances in technology the prospect of international activity is prevalent. To remain ignorant and isolated from this reality will greatly diminish your potential for financial reward and accomplishment. Each year sees the business environment growing by import and export business bring the requirement of communicating with people of different cultures. To not avail oneself of this ability is to greatly limit potential. Be mindful that of the ten top exports for U.S. products, only Canada and Great Britain speak English as a default business language, and their cultures are different.

Even if you never do global business, you will always encounter those in business, either as prospects, customers, or employees, with different cultures and life experience. It will behoove you to master these differences to assure that communication efforts are well received and understood. Such will give you a competitive advantage when dealing with diverse viewpoints and life-experiences.

Diversity is a growing factor in the United States. We are a nation of immigrants and that trend continues today.

However, diversity is not only a factor of immigrants, but also from age, gender, and religion. Diversity either from immigration and other difference create challenges and opportunities in communication. Cultural diversity should affect how messages are composed, sent, received, and understood. Be mindful that these differences include: language, verbal and nonverbal signals, word meaning, time, human relationships. Cultural differences influence the way a sender and a receiver think therefore it affects the way they communicate. It goes beyond words to beliefs, values, and emotions.

Culture is a shared attitude, beliefs, values, expectations, and behavior norms. Realize that you belong to several cultures: your ethic and family group, your religious group, your friends network group, your professional group. All share their own language, customs, habits, and beliefs.

People tend to learn culture from their groups. Group members introduce who you are and how to function in that culture. Culture is passed on from person to person and from generation to generation. This is advantageous for the most part but in a broader context can very well be an obstacle in communicating with other groups and cultures. To achieve maximum success in communicating and business, the entrepreneur must recognize these norms and reconcile what is the best method of communicating to achieve goals.

> *"The World has become small and completely interdependent."*
> Wendell L. Wilkie

When encountering cultural difference communication will be more effective if you adapt your style to that of the culture you are experiencing.

You must:

- Avoid assumptions. Don't assume that others will act the same way that you do, understand the words or language you do, or have the same values and beliefs you have.
- Avoid judgements. When people act or believe differently, don't believe that they are in error or that their way is not as good.
- Acknowledge differences. Don't ignore their differences from your own.
- Be aware and appreciate other cultural differences.
- Write clearly in short messages using simple understandability words.
- Avoid slang and humor, both yours and theirs.
- Ask for feedback to assure understanding.
- Listen carefully and ask for repetition if you don't understand.

CHAPTER NINE

ETHICS

"A business that makes nothing but money is a poor kind of business."
Henry Ford

Ethics is not an easy term to define. In a general sense, ethics is the code of moral principles and values that govern the behavior of a person or group with respect to what is right or wrong. These principles are based cultural, religious, and philosophical beliefs held by us all. They come from our family, friends, school, religion, work, and the media we view and read. These derived ethics values set standards as to what is good or bad in our conduct and decision making. They define how we think and act toward others and how we expect them to think and act toward us. We don't deliberately think of these values, but rather instinctively act based on them. It's only when faced with a compromising situation that raises a moral or ethical dilemma that we may reflect on what is right or wrong. Entrepreneurs and managers of small business particularly have difficulty in maintaining ethical behavior within their organizations. Invariably their operations are more informal and lacking the resources to have sophisticated controls to assure ethical behavior while striving to keep the business alive.

In addition to working the business and attempting to make all the daily decisions necessary to achieve a profitable operation, the entrepreneur manager faces regular ethical decision on (1) individual values, such as integrity and honesty, (2) company values concerning employees well-being,

(3) customer well-being and satisfaction, as reflected in the value provided to the customer, and (4) external responsibilities as to how the business relates to the community and the environment.

Ethical behavior should be a complete organizational concern. Because a company's public communication is the image and representation of the organization, those communications warrant the attention of government to protect the public from misrepresentations. An organization's ethical communication should not be deceptive in any way to prevent harm to the public both without and within the company.

Ethics can be more clearly understood when compared with behaviors governed by laws and by free choices. Human behaviors fall into three categories: codified law, free choice, and ethical behavior.

The first is codified law, in which values and standards are written into the legal system and enforceable in the courts. In this area lawmakers have ruled that people and corporations must behave in a certain way, such as obtaining licenses for cars or paying corporate taxes.

The domain of free choice is at the opposite end of the scale and pertains to behavior about which law has no say and for which an individual or organization enjoys complete freedom. An individual's choice of a marriage partner or religion or a corporation's choice of the number of items to produce is examples of free choice.

Between these domains lies the area of ethics. This area has no specific laws, yet it does have standards of conduct based on shared principles and values about moral conduct that guide an individual or organization. In the domain of free choice, obedience is strictly to oneself. In the domain of codified law, obedience is to laws prescribed by the legal system.

In the ethical behavior domain, obedience is to unenforceable norms and standards about which the individual or organization is aware.

Many individuals and organizations get into trouble with the simplified view that choices are governed by either law or free choice. It leads people to mistakenly assume that if it is not illegal, it must be ethical, as if there were no third domain. A better view is to recognize the domain of ethics and accept moral values as a power for good that can regulate behavior both inside and outside an organization. As the principle of ethics and social responsibility is more widely recognized, companies can use code of ethics and their corporate culture to govern behavior, thereby eliminating the need for additional laws and avoiding the problems of unfettered choice.

Because ethical standards are not codified, disagreements and dilemmas about proper behavior often occur. An ethical dilemma arises in situations when an alternative or behavior is undesirable because of potentially negative ethical consequences. Right or wrong cannot always be clearly identified. Values conflict arise in situations like: Lying is wrong – but what if you lie to protect a loved one? Stealing is wrong – but what if you stole to feed a starving person? Killing is wrong - but what if you killed in self-defense, defending a family member, or in a war?

An action may be legal but is it right, is it ethical? Charging an uninformed customer an exorbitant price may be legal but is it ethical?

We are all familiar and strive to follow the Golden Rule – *"Do unto others as you would have them do unto you."* But what of the lender who practices a different Golden Rule – *"He who has the gold makes the rule."* Most of us believe ourselves to be more ethical than others. But are we, or is such a belief distorted? Is it possible that others may be more ethical if not more so or could we be mistaken about what is ethical and what is not?

How are these conflicts resolved, particularly for the business manager whose goal for success and survival should be to always do what is right for the company and add value for the owners? Many employees hold that unethical behavior and decisions are acceptable if their managers are aware of them. Managers often lead others to unethical behavior by instructing employees to do whatever is necessary to succeed no matter the consequences, that the ends justify the means.

Managers and supervisors faced with ethical choices may benefit from a normative approach, one based on norms and values, to guide their decision making. Normative ethics uses several approaches for guiding ethical decision making. The following four are relevant:

1. Utilitarian Approach – The utilitarian approach holds that moral behavior produces the greatest good for the greatest number. By this method, a decision-maker is expected to consider the effect of decision alternatives on all parties and select the one that optimizes satisfaction

for the greatest number of people. Because optimization to satisfy all can be very complex, simplifying the effort is considered appropriate. Such as a decision that only considers those directly affected and not those that are indirectly affected.

2. Individualism Approach – The individualism approach, also called egoism, contends that acts are moral when they promote the individual's best long-term interests. Individuals calculate the best long-term advantage to themselves as a measure of a decision's goodness. The action that is reached to produce a greater ratio of good to bad for the individual compared to other alternatives is the right one to perform. With everyone pursuing self-interest, the greatest good is ultimately served because people learn to accommodate each other in their own long-term interest. From the viewpoint of Adam Smith, an 18th century economist, in his *Wealth of Nations,* "an individual pursuing his own interests tends to promote the good of his community."

Individualism is believed to lead to honesty and integrity because that works best in the long run. Lying and cheating for immediate self-interest just causes others to lie and cheat in return. Thus, pragmatic individualism ultimately leads to behavior towards others that fits standards of behavior people want towards themselves. Because individualism is easily misinterpreted to support immediate self-gain, it is not popular in highly organized and group-oriented societies. However, individualism is the closest domain to free choice.

3. Moral-Rights Approach – The moral-rights approach asserts that individuals have fundamental rights and liberties that cannot be taken away by another's decision. Therefore, an ethically correct decision is one that best maintains the rights of those affected by it. Such rights are: free consent, privacy, freedom of conscience to refrain from any decision that violates their moral or religious norms, free speech, due process, and the right to life and safety. A decision to eavesdrop on employees would violate the right to privacy, sexual harassment would violate the right to freedom of conscience, and the right of free speech would support whistle-blowers who call attention to illegal or inappropriate actions within an organization.

4. Justice Approach – The justice approach holds that moral decisions must be based on standards of equity, fairness, and impartiality. Distributive justice requires that different treatment of people not

be based on arbitrary characteristics. Individuals that are similar in respect to a decision should be treated similarly. Thus, men and women should not receive different salaries if they are performing the same job. However, people who differ in a substantive way, such as job skills, experience, or responsibility, can be treated differently in proportion to that difference. This differential should have a clear relationship to organizational tasks and goals.

The justice approach is closest to the thinking underlying the domain of law because it assumes that justice is applied through rules and regulations. This application does not require complex calculations such as demanded by the utilitarian approach, nor does it justify self-interest as does the individualism approach. Management is expected to define attributes on which different treatment of employees is acceptable. This approach justifies as ethical behavior efforts to correct past wrongs, playing fair under the rules and insisting on job-relevant differences as the basis for different levels of pay or promotion opportunities. Most present day human resource management is based on the justice approach.

There is nothing in which ethics plays a larger role than in how we communicate. The message we convey should not only be succinct, concise, understandability, but truthful and honest. We will be judged by that standard and the results of that action.

Ethics in Management

> *"Ethics is about how we meet the challenge of doing the right thing when that will cost more than we want to pay."*
> The Josephson Institute of Ethics

When managers are accused of lying, cheating, and stealing, the blame is usually placed on the individual or on the company situation. Most people believe that managers make ethical choices because of individual integrity and honesty, which for the most part is true, but it is not the whole story. The values and culture held in the infrastructure of the organization also shape ethical behavior.

Managers bring specific personality and behavioral traits to the job. Personal needs, family influence, and religious background all shape a manager's value system. Specific personality characteristics such as ego, self-confidence, and a strong sense of independence and internal-locus-of-control may enable managers to make ethical or unethical decisions. It has been suggested that every manager prior to deciding which may have ethical consequences ask himself: How would I feel if my family learned of this decision? How would I feel if this decision was on the front page of the newspaper?

An important personal trait is the three stages of moral development: Preconventional, Conventional, and Principled.

At the preconventional level a manager is concerned with the external rewards and punishment and the concrete personal consequences. At conventional level, while still respecting external rewards and punishments, people learn to conform to the expectations of good behavior as defined by colleagues, friends, family, and society. At the principled level, individuals develop an internal set of standards and values. They will even disobey laws that violate their principles. Internal values and beliefs are more important to them than the expectations of others.

The great majority of managers operate at the conventional level. A few have not advanced beyond pre-conventional and only about 20 percent of American adults reach the principled level of moral development. Individuals at the principled level are able to act in an independent, ethical manner regardless of expectations from others inside or outside the organization. These managers will make ethical decisions whatever the organizational consequences for them.

The values adopted within an organization are important, especially when it is understood that most people operate at the conventional level of moral development believing that their duty is to fulfill obligations and expectations of others. Corporate culture can exert a powerful influence on internal behavior of the organization. Often incidences of theft and kickbacks in a business are found to stem from the historical acceptance of such practices within the organization. Employees were socialized into those values and adopted them as appropriate. In most cases, employees believe that if they do not go along with the ethical values expressed, they will not fit in and their jobs will be at risk.

Corporate culture can be examined to see the kind of ethical signals that are being given to employees. Culture is not the only aspect of an organization that influences ethics, there are others like job satisfaction, trust and loyalty, leadership and decision processes, motivation, promotion and selection processes, but the culture within the organization is the major force because it generates all others and defines company values.

Management methods to improve the ethical work climate and to help the organization to be more responsive to ethical problems include: leading by example, developing a code of ethics, supporting an ethical organizational structure and whistle-blowers, encouraging team cohesiveness and standards of behavior, improving job satisfaction and effective motivation, providing stress and conflict management, and assuring an overall excellence in corporate culture.

Ten Ethical Issues That Most Businesses Face

Ethical dilemmas occur either from internal activities and operations or external operations; and sometimes it is imposed through forces outside the company's control. The following is ten common dilemmas:

1. **Cutting Costs versus Maintaining Quality and Safety**

How to strike a balance between costs, quality, and safety may be the quintessential question in any business. Even when the economy is robust, and sales are high, businesses works hard to keep their cost under control to budget for profit and positive cash-flow. When the economy slows, sales may slack, and the temptation to cut costs even more arises.

A business should always take the long-term view even at the expense of short-term goals. Maintaining quality and safety standards during difficult times may temporarily damage the bottom line but sacrificing quality and safety can lead to bankruptcy.

2. **Overpromising and Under Delivering**

"Actions speak louder than words" may be trite, but it is true. People remember what you do long after they forget what you say. And if you say you'll do something and you don't, people remember that forever.

Overpromising can be tempting especially with start-ups promising impressive returns to investors. Yet, too often, the company doesn't deliver, falling short of meeting customers' needs and investors' expectations. Businesses offering goods and services promises to deliver at a certain time on a certain date. If the promise is broken, you have angry customers and investors.

A business should say straight out, "I don't want to make promises I can't keep." That way you engage the other party in problem solving, and together you may be able to work out a plan that meets everyone's needs.

3. Controlling the Market

Competition can be cutthroat, and business owners and managers are under tremendous pressure to improve sales, cut cost, boost profits, and get a bigger piece of the market. Sometimes businesses react to competition by using unfair practices. And sometimes competitors even conspire to control the market through price fixing.

Resorting to unethical practices most likely will come back to haunt you. Antitrust investigator will no doubt eventually investigate the practice of unethical behavior. Such investigation once made public, even if found not to be illegal will erode consumer confidence and affect sales.

4. Coping with Bad Publicity

The saying that there's no such thing as bad publicity just isn't true. In fact, in these days of social media and the 24-hour news cycle, bad publicity can quickly develop into a public relations nightmare. Recall recent events with Tylenol, Toyota, or British Petroleum.

How bad publicity is handled speaks volumes to the public. If company executives try to ignore or spin the bad news, they simply put off the inevitable and often make the situation worse. If they come across as defensive, angry, or arrogant, they add to the problem.

Transparency, honestly, and accountability are the best antidotes for bad publicity; if handle this way, the story becomes less about the bad news and more about the appropriate response.

5. Being Honest with Consumers

Consumers would rather have bad news delivered straight up than have businesses skirt the real reasons why they can't fulfill consumer needs. As a result, companies need to be truthful with their customers always.

ETHICS

Misleading customers and potential customers, beyond just annoying them, gives them a reason to tell friends and acquaintances to be wary of doing business with you. Potential customers may now avoid you due to your tarnished reputation.

6. **Being Honest with Employees**

The age-old joke among employees is that management treats them like mushrooms. They keep them in the dark and feed them manure. Being honest with employees is the best way for a company to encourage them to be honest with the company.

Being honest isn't always easy for management. When companies have to lay off workers or restructure pay and bonus programs, many managers are tempted to either downplay the changes or react with a "hard-liner-of-take-it-or-leave-it." And sometimes employees seek information that management is not ready to share, the proper response should be, "I can't answer that right now." Telling employees that certain information is confidential currently is always better than lying to them.

7. **Being Honest with Stockholders**

Stockholders naturally want their investments in a company to grow in value. But contrary to what you may think, they don't want growth at any cost. When the situation is a question of doing the right thing versus making money, stockholders likely prefer doing the right thing if the company is as honest and transparent with them as it can be.

When communicating with stockholders, management should always:

> Share Information – Knowledge is power and the more information they have, the more likely they are to understand and approve your decisions.
>
> Be Realistically Hopeful – If going through difficult times acknowledge the challenges being faced and explain what you are doing to meet those challenges. Without overselling, give your investors a reason to look to the future with hope and confidence.
>
> Lead by Example – If you feel like you are not up to the challenge, others can sense it, and they will lose confidence in you and the company. An air of confidence, not arrogance, coupled with

honest and transparent communication, can do more to influence stockholders than any number of quarterly reports.

8. Keeping Accounting Honest

The Sarbanese-Oxley Act (SOX Act) is supposed to make executive officers, auditing firms, and board of directors more accountable for the companies' accounting practices. In real life, the pressures associated with accounting practices haven't changed very much. "Tweaking the numbers" can be tempting when you are looking for new financing, launching an IPO, or wanting to get the analysts and bankers off your back. The temptation increases when salaries, bonuses, and other incentives are tied to meeting financial goals.

9. Lobby for and against Regulation

Even if you are a proprietorship, small partnership, or LLC, as opposed to a large corporation, you must deal with laws and regulations particularly at the local and state level as well as the federal level. Telling lawmakers and government what you think and how laws and regulations affect you is part of being a good businessperson.

To keep governmental communications appropriate;

> Remember who your stakeholders are and what they need and focus on them in your contacts with government officials.
>
> Make your case with facts, not with your personal relationships.
>
> Grease with genuine gratitude, not with cash or gifts.

10. Contributing to Political Campaigns

Giving money to a candidate is a common way for a business to build relationships with elected officials. And nothing about contributing to political campaigns is inherently unethical. But such contributions can blur ethical boundaries when they lead to conflicts of interest.

Make sure you know the limits of campaign contributions, and never pressure employees, vendors, or other stakeholders to support a candidate or campaign.

If you set up a Political Action Committee (PAC), make sure its activities are separate from the business.

Respecting Cultural Difference

One of the toughest ethical questions for multinational businesses is whether they should follow the adage "When in Rome, do as the Romans." Different cultures have different moral norms and practices – a situation know as *cultural relativism*. When multinational companies assume that their moral values (what they ought to do) depend on the culture in which they operate, they practice *ethical relativism*. That is, these companies apply different ethical and moral standards according to the physical locations of their operations.

Companies that do business in the Middle East, for example, must contend with cultural norms that prohibit women from driving or appearing in public without a male escort or without the religious attire (such as head coverings) that their society requires. If your company is committed to gender equality (as it should), how do you live up to your own ethical principles in a culture that places severe restrictions on the activities of women? Do you require your female employees to conform to those cultural rules? Do you avoid hiring women in that culture or deny the women in your company the opportunity to work in your Middle East locations?

The following list three guidelines when doing business in other cultures:

1. **Adhere to universal moral standards.**

The first obligation of any multinational company is to follow *universal moral standards* – the standards that societies develop to survive. Although cultures differ in many of their traditions of what constitutes right and wrong, all societies share some universal moral views. For example, murder is a universal wrong. Some society recognize extenuating factors that may lead you to kill another person, such as defending yourself against an assault, in which case the killing does not meet the definition of murder. But all societies prohibit killing another person for the sake of killing, or in the process of committing another crime. Other universal moral standards include prohibitions against stealing and assault and obligations to care for children and the elderly.

2. **Recognize trust and honesty as basic business standards.**

Multinational companies should adhere to the minimum business standards of trust and honesty. Trust is an essential ingredient of any business transaction. Businesses have to trust suppliers to provide the proper materials or services, and suppliers have to trust their clients to pay them fairly. Workers have to trust their employers to pay them and to protect their safety on the job, and businesses have to trust their employers to do their jobs. Customers have to trust businesses to give them fair value in exchange for the money they pay. Trust is nurture through honest dealings, so honesty is the basic moral currency of any business. Trust and honesty also preclude engaging in bribery or other forms of corruption.

3. **Value human rights.**

Because business depends on economic freedom, multinational businesses should respect basic human liberties. Economic freedom is an element of civil and political liberty, so ethical companies have an obligation to defend and promote human rights wherever they do business. The dilemma for multinational businesses is to walk the fine line between respecting cultural differences and conforming to universal ethical norms.

Developing countries often lack the regulatory structure to ensure that business conforms to the basic moral principles we experience in our own country. And, unfortunately, the absence of an outside monitor can make unethical behavior more tempting, especially if moral breaches would increase revenues or profits. In the information age of instant news and viral videos, a company runs a serious risk of exposure by flouting universal moral standards. Even if government regulators aren't watching, human rights groups and the news media are. And public opinion can deliver a severe blow to a company's reputation, and to its profits.

Ethics in Leadership

> *"Ethics is a code of values which guide our choices and actions and determine the purpose and course of our lives."*
> Ayn Rand

In improving organizational ethical behavior no role is more crucial than that of senior management visible commitment to ethical conduct. It must give constant leadership in renewing and enforcing the ethical values of the organization. The commitment must be actively communicated in speeches, directives, company publications, and especially in actions which set the tone of the organization.

In resolving ethical problems as in solving all problems managers should: analyze the consequences, analyze the actions, and decide.

1. Analyze the consequences – Who will be helped by what you do? Who will be harmed? What kind of help and harm is involved? What will be the result in the long run as well as the short run?

2. Analyze the action – consider the options from a different viewpoint. What are the different consequences? How do they measure against moral principles like fairness, equality, honesty, integrity, and respect for others? What is the common good?

3. Decide – View all perspectives and decide and evaluate the results. Alter your actions if called for.

Code of Ethics

A code of ethics is a formal statement of the company's values concerning ethics and social issues; it communicates to employees what the company stands for and how it should behavior. When a code of ethics is written, employees tend to take it more seriously and accept that management also considers it very important. Having such a written system in place is the best well to stop ethical problems before they start. Codes of ethics tend to exist in two types: Principle-Based statements and Policy-Based statements.

Principle-Based statements are designed to affect corporate culture, define fundamental values, and contain general language about company responsibilities, quality of products and service, and treatment of employees. These general statements of principle are often call corporate credos.

Policy-Based statements generally outline the procedure to be used in specific ethical situations such as: marketing practice, conflict of interest, observance of laws, proprietary information, political gifts, and equal opportunities.

Codes of ethics state the values and behaviors that are expected and those that will not be tolerated within the organization. They must have full management support to assure that the code will be meaningful and followed.

A well-written code of ethics should establish several things. It can state what the company expects and understands what is and is not ethical behavior, a values statement. It can establish a clear and detailed guide to acceptable behavior. It can articulate exact policies of behavior for specific situations. And, it can outline what punishments and reprimands will be forthcoming for violations.

Before a company can create a code of ethics that everyone can respect and adhere to, it needs to be relevant to the organization and industry and have a foundation on what a code of ethics is. The best ethics codes have the following:

Apply to everyone:

From the newest hire to the board of directors, every person in the company is expected to adhere to the code. And just as important, everyone is subject to the same disciplinary measures for violating the code, regardless of position in the company.

Are consistent, even when the market isn't:

When economic pressures increase, compliance with the company's ethical code can easily decrease. However, the company that compromises its ethics to survive a slump risks both its reputation and its future. A dynamic, living code of ethics is relevant in boom and bust times.

Promote transparency and accountability:

"Sunlight is said to be the best of disinfectants; electric light the most efficient policeman." The less secretive the procedures and policies are, the less opportunity employees have for skirting or ignoring the rules. Less opportunity for unethical conduct means less temptation to indulge in questionable behavior.

Keep up with the times:

This means applying core values to new developments in technology, regulation, and any other conditions that affect the employee's on-the-job conduct.

Ethical Structure:

Ethical structure represents the various systems, positions, and programs a company can undertake to implement ethical behavior.

An ethics committee is a group of executives appointed to oversee company ethics. The committee provides ruling on questionable ethical issues. The committee assumes responsibility for disciplining violators of the code, which is essential to directly influence employee behavior. The ethics committee will generally report directly to the Board-of-Directors.

A senior executive, reporting to the CEO, may serve as an ethical ombudsman given the responsibility of corporate conscience that hears and investigates ethical complaints and indicates potential ethical failure to top management prior to the necessity of full committee action.

Other effective structures are formal ethics training programs and "hot" lines availability.

Ethics training seeks to help people understand the ethical aspects of decisions and to incorporate high ethical standards into their daily activities. Ethics training programs require all employees to attend an orientation session and on-going seminars at which they read and sign-off on the corporate code of ethics. Executives are providing training in ethical decision-making.

A "hot" line is a toll-free number to which employees can confidentially report questionable behavior as well as possible fraud, waste, or abuse. No reprisals will be taken against anyone using it.

Ethics and Technology

"Big Brother is watching you."
George Orwell

Advances in technology have greatly enhanced the efficiency, effectiveness, and productivity of business. The computer, internet, e-mail, instant messaging, fax, cell-phones all have made communication of information and product delivery more assessable to employees and customers alike. With such ease of use and available has also produced perhaps a loss of privacy. As a customer and even a medical patient, your records are easily obtained by others, often by the very companies you are doing business with to lower their cost. As an employee, your e-mail and web-site visited are no doubt being monitored as is your business phone to assure your work productivity.

Google and other search engines keep records of our individual searches, why?

Many internet-based businesses acquire personal information which their privacy policy declares that they won't sell to third parties but only used to assist you. Purchase a book on the web and more than likely, the book sellers will advise you of previous purchases and recommend similar material.

As an employee of a business, your productivity during work hours represents your work obligation for pay you owe the company. Therefore, your actions during that time are at the discretion of the company. Other than lunch or other breaks, all your activity should be work related, and any monitoring should not be regarded as an infringement of your privacy. If you want to do something in private don't do it at work.

Many employees take the position that whereas the time at work does represent the fulfillment of an obligation for which compensation is received, however this obligation should not intrude on individual civil rights. I am an employee not a servant and as such should be notified of any surveillance and monitoring. Why should all suffer for the violations of a few? Such monitoring implies that I cannot be trusted; if not then why was I hired.

Ethical Accounting Issues in Business

"Earnings can be as pliable as putty when a charlatan heads the company reporting them."
Warren Buffet

An ethical issue in business is a problem, situation, or opportunity that requires an individual decision maker, group of people, or organization to choose among alternative actions that must be evaluated as (the better) right or (the lesser) wrong, ethical or unethical.

It has been said that there is no such thing as "business" ethics. That a single standard of ethics applies to both our business and to our personal lives. Remember, that it is individuals that manage businesses and it is individuals that make decisions for those businesses.

While most recognize that business must earn a profit to survive; it is the steps taken by those individuals running the business to make a profit that concerns ethicists. The "ends do not justify the means". If it did, business could rationalize not taking the necessary steps to protect the environment based on excessive costs to comply with the EPA laws. If a company via the decisions of its managers takes such a position, it would be placing its own self-interests, perhaps in the guise of maximizing shareholder wealth, ahead of the interest of society.

Five major ethical issues have been identified: honesty and fairness, conflicts of interest, fraud, discrimination, and information technology.

With an emphasis on business transactions in accounting producing accurate and reliable financial statements and transparency of events, focused is placed on the first three.

Honesty and Fairness

Abraham Lincoln once said, *"No man has a good enough memory to be a successful liar."* A person who lies about a matter then must remember what was said and be sure to provide a consistent response when questioned; otherwise the story will come apart.

You have an obligation to be honest and trustworthy in your business dealings as well as your personal life. What kind of example do you set for your family; sons and daughters, if you do improper things in business while touting ethical behavior at home in your personal life.

Fairness, of course, is the treatment of others equally in ethical decision making. Fairness is not often regarding in accounting or financial reporting, but it too requires objective disclosures with the interests of its stakeholders. These include the stockholders, creditors, employees, suppliers, customers, and government agencies that regulate business. Accounting professionals should approach their roles as preparers of financial statements without bias of how transactions should be reported and disclosed. The statements should be transparent: accurate, reliable, and reflect full disclosure; and, of course, should be prepared in accordance with GAAP and not be misleading.

Conflict of Interests

A conflict of interest is a situation in which private interest or personal considerations could affect or be perceived to affect an employee's judgment to act in the best interests of the business. Examples include using an employee's position, confidential information, or personal relationship for private gain or advancement.

Objectivity and integrity are essential qualities for employees of any organization. It is the perception that a person may be influenced by matters or relationships not relevant to a decision that creates many of the conflicts of interest problems in business. When such occurs creating a conflict of interest, one should step aside or recuse himself from the matter and avoid the appearance of bias. (A member of the Supreme Court should have done so regarding the Obamacare debate as she was instrumental in its development prior to her appointment to the Supreme Court.)

Honest people not only avoid lying but also have as a goal the disclosure of all information that another party has a right to know (lying by omission).

FRAUD

Fraud can be defined as a deliberate misrepresentation to gain an advantage over another party.

The Association of Certified Fraud Examiners (ACFE) defines occupational fraud as "the use of one's occupation for personal enrichment through the deliberate misuse or misapplication of the employing organization's resources or assets."

ACFE identifies four key elements of fraud schemes: the activity is clandestine; the activity violates the perpetrator's fiduciary responsibilities; the act is committed for direct or indirect personal financial benefit; and it costs the business assets or revenue. These schemes occur because of a lack of internal controls and ineffective corporate governance.

Fraud occurs because of a failure in organizational ethics because financial statement fraud cannot occur without the involvement of top management and either a breakdown or override of internal controls. In these organizations, the tone set by top management does not promote ethical behavior, and the result is increased pressure on accountants and auditors to detect and report the fraud.

Whistle-Blowers

> *"The word whistle-blower suggests that you're a tattletale or that you're somehow disloyal... But I wasn't disloyal in the least bit. People were dying. I was loyal to a higher order of ethical responsibility."*
> Dr. Jeffrey Wigand

Employees' disclosure of illegal, immoral, or illegitimate practices on the employer's part is called whistle-blowing. A whistleblower exposes the misdeeds of others in the organization. Anyone in the organization can blow the whistle if he or she detects such organizational activity. Whistle-blowers often report wrongdoing to outsiders, such as regulatory agencies, law enforcement, newspapers, and senators or representatives. In enlightened companies that strive for ethical behavior, whistle-blowers are able to report internally to an ethic ombudsman or ethics committee.

Whistle-blowers must be protected if this is to be an effective safeguard, otherwise, they will suffer, and the organization may continue its unethical or illegal activity. Federal and state laws offer whistleblowers defense against potential retaliatory action from organizations accused. However legal protection can still be inadequate. Laws vary from state to state, and federal laws mainly protect government workers in their efforts to report misdeeds in government agencies. Within the organization, whistleblowers may still encounter difficulties by a strict chain of command that makes it hard to bypass the boss; a strong work group identity that encourages loyalty; and ambiguous priorities that make it hard to distinguish right from wrong. It has been observed that the top reasons for not reporting wrongdoings are; the belief that no corrective action would be taken, and the fear of retaliation by the revelation not being kept confidential.

Cohesiveness

Cohesiveness is another important aspect of creating and managing an ethical work climate and corporate culture. Employee team cohesiveness is the extent to which members are attracted to the team and its effort, and motivated to remain in it and contribute. Members of highly cohesive teams are committed to team activities and projects, attend and participate in meetings, and are happy and satisfied when the team succeeds. Members of less cohesive teams are less concerned about the team's accomplishments and welfare.

The characteristics of an organization's structure, context, and corporate culture influence team cohesiveness.

First is the interaction between the employees of the organization. The greater the amount of contact among employees and the more time spend together, the more cohesive the organization. Through frequent and productive interaction employees get to know one another fostering better cooperation and become more devoted to the objectives and goals of the organization.

Second is the concept of shared goals. If the employees agreed on the goals of the organization and its vision, they will more cohesive in a team effort. Agreeing on the purpose and direction of the organization binds them together.

Third is the personal attraction each has to the organization. They desire to be with others who share in similar attitudes and values to accomplish common goals and enjoy being together in achieving that task. Competition with another organization is also a factor in increasing cohesiveness of an organization as, with a team effort, it strives to win. When the success and favorable evaluation of the winning effort is recognized by senior management and outsiders greatly adds to the pride, job satisfaction, commitment, and cohesiveness of the organization as the team members feel good with their accomplishment.

The outcome of the cohesiveness of an organization can fall into two categories: morale and productivity.

Generally, morale is higher in cohesive companies because of increased communication, a friendly climate, commitment and loyalty to the organization, and employees' participation in organization decisions, activities, and objectives.

Cohesiveness may have several effects; first, employee's productivity tends to be more uniform. Productivity difference among employees is small because the team exerts pressure on each other towards conformity.

In addition, cohesive organizations have the potential and tendency to be more productive with the degree of productivity efficiency related to the relationship between management and the working team.

Behavior Norms

Norms of the organization is a standard of conduct that is shared by the employees and guides their behavior. Norms are informal and often part of the corporate culture. They are not written down as are rules, regulations, and procedures. They are valuable to an organization as they define the boundaries of acceptable behavior. Norms make work performance easier for employees as they provide a frame of reference of what is right or wrong and expected behavior for key values and company survival. They began to develop in the very first interaction among employees.

Ethical Principles for Entrepreneurs:

(*Ethical Obligations and Opportunities in Business Ethical Decision Making,* Josphenson Institute of Ethics.Los Angeles, CA)

The following list of principles incorporates the characteristics and values associated with ethical behavior.

1. HONESTY: Ethical entrepreneur managers are honest and truthful in all their dealings and they do not deliberately mislead or deceive others by misrepresentations, overstatements, partial truths, selective omissions, or any other means.

2. INTERGRITY: Ethical entrepreneurs demonstrate personal integrity and the courage of their convictions by doing what they think is right even when there is great pressure to do otherwise; they are principled, honorable, and upright; they

will fight for their beliefs. They will not sacrifice principle for expediency or be hypocritical or unscrupulous.

3. PROMISE-KEEPING AND TRUSTWORTHINESS: Ethical entrepreneurs are worthy of trust, they are candid and forthcoming in supplying relevant information and correcting misapprehensions of fact, and they make every reasonable effort to fulfill the letter and spirit of their promises and commitments. They do not interpret agreements in an unreasonably technical or legalistic manner to rationalize noncompliance or create justification for escaping their commitments.

4. LOYALTY: They are worthy of trust, demonstrate fidelity and loyalty to persons and institutions by friendship in adversity, and display support and devotion to duty; they do not use or disclose information learned in confidence for personal advantage. They safeguard the ability to make independent professional judgments by scrupulously avoiding undue influences and conflicts of interest. They are loyalty to their employees and colleagues. They respect the proprietary information of former employers and refuse to engage in any activities that take undue advantage of their previous positions.

5. FAIRNESS: Ethical entrepreneurs are fair and just in all dealings; they do not exercise power arbitrarily, and do not use overreaching nor indecent means to gain or maintain any advantage nor take undue advantage of another's mistake or difficulties. Fair persons manifest a commitment to justice, the equal treatment of individuals, and tolerance for and acceptance of diversity and are open-mined, they are willing to admit they are wrong and, when appropriate, change their positions and beliefs.

6. CONCERN FOR OTHERS: They are caring, compassionate, benevolent, and kind; they live the Golden Rule, help those-in-need, and seek to accomplish their business objectives in a manner that causes the least harm and the greatest positive good.

7. RESPECT FOR OTHERS: Ethical entrepreneur managers demonstrate respect for the human dignity, autonomy, privacy, rights, and interests of all those who have a stake in their decisions; they are courteous and treat all people with equal respect and dignity regardless of sex, race, or national origin.

8. LAW ABIDING: They abide by laws, rules, and regulations relating to their business.

9. COMMITMENT TO EXCELLENCE: Ethical entrepreneurs pursue excellence in performing their duties, are well informed and prepared, and constantly endeavor to increase their proficiency in all areas of responsibility.

10. LEADERSHIP: Ethical entrepreneurs are conscious of the responsibilities and opportunities of their position of leadership and seek to be positive ethical role model by their own conduct and by helping to create an environment in which principled reasoning and ethical decision making are highly prized.

11. REPUTATION AND MORALE: They seek to protect and build the company's good reputation and the morale of its employees by engaging in no conduct that might undermine respect and by taking whatever actions are necessary to correct or prevent inappropriate conduct of others.

12. ACCOUNTABILITY: Ethical entrepreneur managers acknowledge and accept personal accountability for the ethical quality of their decisions and omissions to themselves, their employees, their colleagues, their companies, and their communities.

COMMON OBSTACLES TO ETHICAL ENTREPRENEUR BEHAVIOR

"If ethics are poor at the top, that behavior is copied down through the organization."
Robert Noyce

GREED

Greed is defined as "a selfish and excessive desire for more of something than is needed." "Personal Greed" appears as the main factor in the ethics scandals of the early 2000s. Even though most business executives are basically ethical, there is tremendous pressure to create profits which could lead to "ethically vulnerability" encouraging questionable activity.

Greed isn't always about money. Sometimes people are greedy for power, status, influence, or anything else they desire in excess.

So, for a business to attempt to keep greed in check, the following should be exercised:

Establish an ethical culture that puts principle ahead of profits

Set up a system of checks and balances that promote accountability and transparency

Set up a reward system that combines financial and other incentives to do good, not just to do well.

GROUP-THINKING

Group-thinking is the failure to invite, recognize, or listen to different points of view. It is tough to overcome because group thinkers can intimidate the people who might present different viewpoints in a number-of-ways. i.e. If managers display a don't-tell-me-anything-I-don't-want-to hear attitude, or if they react with anger when someone expresses an opinion that's different from theirs, chances are they'll seldom get any valuable input from the people around them.

TUNNEL VISION

Tunnel vision is closely related to group-thinking in that both conditions involve not paying attention to differing viewpoints and ignoring relevant details. While group-thinking typically occurs when contemplating a specific action, tunnel vision can make you stay committed to a course of action even when you should abandon it.

Tunnel vision is most common when the corporate culture doesn't make allowance for failure. Business is risky by nature, and expecting unbroken success is unrealistic. Nevertheless, many managers feel enormous pressure to always be successful, and sometimes they are so focused on that goal that they don't even realize that they are crossing ethical lines to achieve it.

SELF-INTEREST

Most people tend to do what will benefit them and avoid what may harm them. But often strong motivated self-interest can tug people toward unethical behavior.

Motivated self-interest can stem from any number of needs, desires, or goals including:

> Fear of losing a job
> Desire for more pay
> Desire for status, power, or influence

ARROGANCE

Every business leader needs confidence, but, all too often, confidence develops into arrogance- the belief that you are smarter, more visionary, and righter than those around you. Arrogant people don't tolerate dissent, and they dismiss questions and alternative viewpoints as unworthy of consideration. They firmly believe that they are superior to everyone else and that, because they are better than everyone else, they can do whatever they want.

LABOR COSTS

Hiring workers is expensive, and labor is always a target item when companies have to trim the budget. The temptation to focus on costs and ignore inconvenient facts about your workers' conditions can be powerful.

PRODUCTION COSTS

Even if you can get cheap labor without violating ethical standards, the cost of materials, equipment, and space can easily be astronomical. And when production costs encroach on profits, the pressure to reduce those costs can be overwhelming. The temptation to shave these costs often results in less quality, employee morale, and customer satisfaction which will impact profits even more.

LACK OF TRANSPARENCY

Transparency is simply making information available to both employees and customers. The more open a company is about its operations, the less likely it is to suffer from ethical nearsightedness.

FEAR

Fear is a double-edged sword when it comes to business ethics. On the one-hand, it can help people fight the temptation to behave unethically because they fear the consequences of getting caught: feeling embarrassed or humiliated, disappointing relatives and friends, going to jail, and so on. But, on the other hand, if this is the only reason they behave ethically, then the business has a corporate culture and management problem.

DOUBLE STANDARDS

Managers who take a "do as I say, not as I do" approach to supervising surrender the most valuable currency they have in promoting ethical behavior: their own integrity. Employees who don't respect their managers can become cynical and even retaliatory by stealing time, supplies, or money, or by otherwise sabotaging the company.

The same issues arise when management ignores ethical violations from high performers but punish the same infractions from average or low-performing employees. The message is: "You can do whatever you want as long as you make money for the company."

Ethical Guidepost

Rotary Club, a worldwide organization of business and professional leaders, has set a high standard for business conduct. It calls on its members to ask the following four questions when they prepare to decide about the things they think, say, or do:

1. **Is it the Truth?**
2. **Is it Fair to all concerned?**

3. **Will it build Goodwill and Better Friendships?**
4. **Will it be Beneficial to all concerned?**

In addition to these four the following ten rules should be followed:

Ten Ethical Guideposts

1. **Respect All People**

Regardless of differences (or similarities) in skin color, religious beliefs, or any other area of life, every individual is an autonomous agent capable of making his or her own decisions about what's right and wrong. When you respect others' autonomy, you don't view them as a means to an end and are more likely to treat them fairly.

Helpful tips to respect others:

> Mind your manners. Saying "please" and "thank you" isn't just common courtesy; these words are an implicit acknowledgement of the other person's individuality.
> Invite Opinions. When you ask others what they think, you place them on an equal footing as people – even if they aren't equals in your business.
> Give credit where it's due. Anyone can work hard and generate good ideas, no matter what their job title. But the managers who take credit for their employees' efforts undermine the employees' standing as individuals deserving respect. Take pride in the people on your team whom you may have very well assembled, brag about them, their efforts and ideas. You will be surprised how much your own reputation will shine.

2. **Don't Lie**

Telling the truth is a universal ethical standard because societies can't function if lying is okay. Commerce would grind to a halt because consumers wouldn't be able to trust businesses.

On the other hand, sometimes telling the whole truth goes against the company's best interest. You don't have to lie to avoid telling the whole truth. Be honest with information you can release, and, for information you can't share, say, "I'm not at liberty to discuss this particular issue."

3. **Avoid Bribes**

Every country in the world officially outlaws bribery for one simple reason: Bribery creates an unequal playing field that disproportionately penalizes small companies and poor people. Bribery basically is offering to exchange something-usually money-in return for an unfair advantage in some aspect of business, such as bidding on contracts.

Giving one bribe cam make your company vulnerable to repeated demands for "gifts" to receive the permits you need to do business. Staunch refusal to bribery demands keeps your company's reputation clean and lowers the pressure to "play the game" in areas where bribery is commonplace.

4. **Don't Make a Mess**

For decades, companies spewed pollutants into the air, water, and soil without a second thought. But these days, companies have an ethical obligation, and sound business reasons, to ensure that their activities are eco-friendly.

From an ethical viewpoint, protecting the environment is good business because good corporate citizens strive to improve the communities they operate in, generating benefits for everyone. If your operation employs people but makes the water undrinkable, you aren't helping the community nor your very employees and consumers who are essential to your operation.

Often, especially due to government mandates, cleaning up messes is more expensive (and more damaging to your reputation and future sales) than avoiding them in the first place.

5. **If You Make a Mess, Clean It Up**

Accidents can happen, even if you're careful about you conduct. Messes can be physical, such as oil spills or asbestos in buildings. But messes can also arise from simple human interaction- ranging from innocent misunderstandings to outright bad behavior. Whatever causes the mess and whatever kind of mess it is, you still need to clean it up.

> You don't have to do the cleanup alone; asking for help is okay if you take responsibility for your part in making the mess. But leaving the mess for someone else to take care of is unacceptable.

6. Take Responsibility for Your Actions

Nobody likes to watch the companies play the blame game. Unfortunately, owning up to mistakes can cost a fortune in government fines and civil lawsuits, too many companies have forgotten the value of combining a sincere apology with a genuine effort to correct the problem.

Taking responsibility involves the following four steps:

1. Acknowledge the problem
2. Offer a sincere apology
3. Repair the damage
4. Take steps to avoid repeating the problem.

5. Play by the Rules

Sometimes rules are silly and ineffective. But even if they are, most rules are intended to make sure everyone has the same opportunities. Breaking the rules violates the universal ethical standards of honesty and trust, and no business (or society) can survive for long without those acceptable standards. The ethical way to cope with rules that don't make sense is to work to change them, not to break them.

6. Work Hard

Working hard is how you ensure that you earn your rewards. Most ethical theories and religions hold that hard work enhances your character and is morally beneficial, while laziness is typically reviled. The concept of a *meritocracy* (a society in which effort and achievement are rewarded with more money, status, or both) places its highest premium on working hard and smart.

Working hard means:

> Consistently giving your best efforts at your job every day;
>
> Showing up on time and putting in a full day's work;
>
> Using your skills and talents to advance both the company's interests and your own

This does not imply that leisure is bad; everyone needs some leisure time to take care of themselves physically, mentally, emotionally, and spiritually. However, when at work, your employer and your fellow employees deserve your full attention and commitment.

7. **Be Humble in Success**

Celebrate your wins, but don't get cocky. Remember, success in business is always a team effort, coupled with good fortune. If you start believing your own hype, you end up arrogant and blind to situations that can threaten your business.

You can take pride in your achievements. But don't allow pride to interfere with your vision to see both threats and opportunities, nor interfere with your dedication to doing things right and doing the right thing.

8. **Be Generous**

Generosity is more than just writing a check to your favorite charity. A generous spirit comes from an attitude of abundance – a focus on what you have rather on what you don't have. Generosity allows you to feel joy at other's accomplishments and good fortune, to forgive colleagues for their human fragilities and mistakes, and to empathize with those whose circumstance are less pleasant than yours.

Generosity also enables you to offer help for the sake of helping (not because you can get good publicity from it) and to motivate your employees to do their best work. Your generosity provides an example for others to cultivate a generous spirit, helping to create a company culture in which success is measured by ethical behavior as well as profits.

How to Keep the Company Ethical

Choose Ethical Leaders

Hiring ethical managers may be the single most important thing you can do to build and maintain an ethical culture. If your company's leaders aren't committed to ethical behavior, all your other attempts- establishing a code of ethics, applying ethical standards to everyone, having an independent board of directors- are likely to have limited impact. Why; because employees have no respect for a "do as I say, not as I do" manager.

So how do you choose ethical leaders? By asking probing questions during the interview process, such as:

> Describe a workplace dilemma encountered and explain how resolved.
>
> Pose a hypothetical ethical dilemma and ask how they would handle it.
>
> Ask an opinion on current business ethics in the news.

Have an Independent Board of Directors

The board of directors is responsible for ensuring the organization's future, creating the policies and objectives, and appointing the managers who administer the policies and implement the objectives. Also, they have a responsibility to the stockholders.

Boards of directors don't do enough in probing and questioning management's decisions to make sure they're ethical and in the company's best interest. Sometimes directors are more interested in what they can gain than in what's best for the company. Sometimes they have conflicts of interest that hamper their ability to make good decisions. Most boards:

Rely on management to keep them informed.

Often don't have the time and sometimes the skills or background to understand complex transactions or other details of the company's business.

Foster a "go along to get along" mind-set that discourages questioning of a company's actions or performance.

Have a Living Code of Ethics

Codes of ethics are often posted prominently for everyone to see. Unfortunately, they often spend their existence gathering dust. One of the keys in keeping your company ethical is making sure your code of ethics isn't just a forgotten piece of paper. It should be a dynamic, living document, continually reviewed for relevance and reinforced through training, managerial example, and self-policing among employees.

Explain the Reasoning behind the Code

Knowledge is power, and the easiest way to get employees to adhere to the code is to explain why the code the code is important. New hires are too often asked to sign off on the code but then never think about it again.

Apply Ethical Standards to Everyone

Nothing saps morale and commitment to ethical conduct more quickly than the perception that different rules apply to different people. Most will accept that those in positions of authority get paid more. But very few believe it is okay to hold different people to different ethical standards.

Value Ethics over Performance

Often higher-performing workers aren't held to the same ethical rules as poor performers.

Engage Stakeholders

To engage stakeholders a company has to figure how to communicate with them and how to encourage them to communicate with your company. The more communications established, the more successful will be needed input to maintain the company's ethical culture.

Support Industry-Wide Regulation

Companies that sincerely promote sensible regulation gets an image boost that can translate into new customers and higher revenues. Your stakeholders want to be proud of their association with your company, and by supporting ways to ensure and enforce ethically standards; you show stakeholders that your company is genuinely committed to doing the right thing.

Create an Environment Where People Want to Come to Work

Employees who feel valued, who are paid a fair wage, and who feel that they have a voice and an important contribution to make are far less likely to resort to ethical lapses.

Stay Alert to Ethical Threats

Creating and maintain an ethical culture is not a one-shot deal; it requires long-term commitment and integration into the overall business strategy. Regular training and review of ethical policies and procedures, combined with input from stakeholders, are essential elements of your strategy.

> "...there is one and only one social responsibility of business-to use its resources and engage in activities designed to increase its profits so long as it stays within the rules of the game, which is to say, engages in open and free competition without deception or fraud."
> Milton Friedman, "Capitalism and Freedom"

CHAPTER TEN

MARKETING

"Genius is one per cent inspiration and ninety-nine per cent perspiration."
Thomas Alva Edison

A vital communication without the company is that to secure customers and promote the image and reputation of the organization.

Marketing is everything you do to promote your product and everything that interacts with your customers. Marketing is the delivery of customer satisfaction at a profit. It is the process of developing, pricing, promoting, and distributing goods, services, and ideas to satisfy the needs and wants of customers. The entrepreneur must look at all aspects of the business from a marketing point of view and not just from an operational or product standpoint. This is often very difficult for an entrepreneur starting a business as he/she did not go into business to be a salesperson and may be more comfortable with the operational and product aspects of the venture. They will quickly realize that marketing the company is a continuous effort. To be most effective and productive, it should be done daily and be involved in all areas of the business.

The marketing part (Appendix A-1) of your Business Plan describes how you will attempt to create and maintain customers for a profit. You need to describe your industry, your market, your competition, your prospective customers, your marketing mix, your method of distribution, and what you plan to be your competitive advantage.

Our free-enterprise system encourages competition. This means it is a buyer's market rather than a seller's. You must be customer oriented rather than simply product oriented. If you do not offer what the market desires and you are no better than your competition, then you will fail. People do business with people they know, like, and trust. It is your task to ensure that everything you do and say will cause customers and potential customers to know you better, like and trust you more.

It is common for the entrepreneur to focus on the product rather than the customer. Remember, you must be customer oriented and not product oriented. Get to know the customer and provide the customer value that they want. To measure customer satisfaction, you must constantly strive to get feedback from the customer. Be mindful that –

> You will never hear from 95% of unhappy customers,
>
> 85% of those unhappy customers will not buy from you again,
>
> For every complaint you receive, on average there will be another 25 you have not heard,
>
> If you resolve the complaint, 75% of them will do business with you again,
>
> The average unhappy customer tells ten people about the problem with you,
>
> Most customers that leave a business do so due to indifference- something you can control.

To succeed, your business must offer what your competitors don't offer at all and/or provide better customer service. You must provide potential customers a good reason to bypass your competition and come to you. You must offer customer value that includes quality, price, convenience, and before and after the sale service. You need to offer what people want to buy, not what you want to sell them. Customers do not buy what you like, they buy what they want. Instead of trying to start a business in search of customers, listen to the market and find customers in search of a business.

The marketing part of the business plan begins with the identification of customers' wants that are not being met at all or well enough. You will need to research the market and the specific geographic area you have selected.

You need to know about the population, the level and rate of business activity growth, what are the major employees and are they doing well. In general, what are the business conditions of your market area? You are trying to identify the number of potential customers, who they are, how often they buy, who they are currently buying from, how much they spend, and if they are brand or store loyal. Getting customers is half of the battle. Keeping them is the other half. Do not be product oriented and only sell products or service; but be customer oriented and sell satisfaction. You have not obtained customers unless they come back for more products and that they talk favorable about you and your business to others. Always be aware that the average business losses one third of its customer base each year either due to their death, moving away, or switching to a competitor.

Now that you have analyzed the market, determined the strengths and weaknesses of the existing businesses, and identified your target customers, you are able to develop your marketing mix. The marketing mix represents your way of creating and maintaining customers for a profit. It reflects what you plan to do for a competitive advantage and how you will be able to offer greater satisfaction and value to your customers than your competition.

The marketing mix consists of four components, the four P's., these are Product and service strategy, Price strategy, Promotional strategy, and Physical distribution strategy.

The four C's of the marketing mix are Customer Solution and Satisfaction, Customer Cost, Convenience, and **Communication.**

The marketing mix represents your way of creating and maintaining customers for a profit.

One of the basic principles for business success is, "To succeed, you must be better than your competition, "To be better, you must be different." Your marketing mix must be better than your competition in areas your target market values.

Being different does not automatically mean you will be better. Your market offering is better only if your target market considers it to be better. Better means your market values it and is willing to pay for it. Therefore, you must be in tune with your potential customers and that you try to see the world through their eyes.

A business must be tailored to the needs, desires, interests, preferences, and behaviors of their target market. Your target market is the judge and jury when your business goes on trial in the marketplace. You may believe you have the lowest prices in town, but if your target market is price-sensitive and believes (their perception) you are not the lowest, then they will go elsewhere. The same applies to your location, delivery system and other components of your market mix offering.

The target market will most likely be the primary market that will purchase your products and services. Your secondary market will consist of those purchasers outside the target market and will require a different market strategy.

Product/Service Strategy

Each component of the marketing mix plays an integral role in your effort to create and maintain customers. Product/service strategy may play the most significant role. Businesses are usually described in terms of the kind of products and service they offer. Pricing, advertising, and physical distribution are also important. But, if the product you offer is not what people want, then it will not matter how low your prices are, how catchy your advertising, or if you are convenient located.

Pricing Strategy

There are two ways of marketing: (1) Saturate the market with your message- may be effective but very expensive; and (2) Innovative marketing in a dollar conscious manner.

The second choice is often the only option available to small business owners on a limited budget. However, it can be very effective but cost conscious without being innovative is just being cheap and will often not be very effective. Many businesses have adopted a percentage of sales approach to spending on marketing. This may be a good benchmark for cost but all spending most mindful to contribute towards the goal. It has been said that half of all money spent on advertisement is wasted; the problem is the business does not know what half. The objective, particularly for a new small business, is not to waste any.

MARKETING

Your pricing strategy will depend on numerous factors. Prices will need to reflect the target market you select, the nature and extent of competition, the strength of your location, your cost structure, and the type of product you will offer. There may be as many approaches to pricing as there are factors that affect a business's pricing strategy.

The Standard Markup Approach or "cost-based approach" is used by many businesses. The standard markup means that a business will base its selling price on what the product costed the business plus a percentage of that cost. The percentage added to the cost is known as the markup.

Selling price = cost + markup

The percentage of markup may be suggested by your suppliers or it could be based on other cost-related factors. Recognize that it must be competitive, or your product will not sell without some other perception of added value that is better than competition (premium product). If you cannot be competitive and do not have a premium product that customers want and are willing to pay for then you do not have a business.

The Match-the- Market Approach resembles the standard markup approach.

Businesses that compete against one another may offer similar products, perhaps even the same product from the same suppliers, at comparable prices. If so, what will clearly make the difference is in superior service and delivery. A primary drawback is that if you have a competitive advantage valued by your market, then you should be able to charge higher prices. The match-the-market approach is a "play it safe approach" that fails to consider your unique strengths.

Promotional Strategy and Physical Distribution Strategy

Promotional strategy can be viewed as how you communicate with your customers. Physical distribution refers to how you get your product to them.

Promotional strategy includes advertising, publicity, sales promotion, personal selling, and public relations. Your promotional strategy must address the: who, what, when, where, and how much money to spend.

The most common media used to advertise are: Newspapers, Television, Radio, Magazines, The Internet, Direct Mail, and Outdoor Billboards.

Physical distribution represents the way you provide products to your customers. If the customers are to come to you, then your location and facility is important. The location decision is like going fishing- You should find out where the fish are and fish there. Many businesses fail because the location was convenient for the owners but not for the potential customers.

Offering your goods or services to charities is an excellent way to gain exposure and give back to the community at the same time.

In addition to the Marketing Section in your Business Plan (appendix A-1); the following should be considered:

RESEARCH PHASE

1. **Define your concept**

    What business are you really in?
    List your products or services
    Define you market position
    Define your target market and how will you reach it.
    Define your desired image

2. **Your business image**

    What business do your customers think you are in?
    What are they buying?
    What compliments or complaints do you get?
    What sells you?

3. **Understand your market**

    Market size
    Trends
    Economic Environment
    Technological changes
    Political/Legal changes
    Social/Culture environment
    Demographic changes
    Resources
    Skills
    Substitute markets

4. **Know your competition**
   > Who are they?
   > Identify strengths/weakness
   > Market share

5. **Know your customer**
   > Identify needs, wants, and desires
   > Customer profile
   > Demographics

STRATEGIC PHASE

1. **Product/Service**

2. **Distribution**

3. **Location**

4. **Pricing**

5. **Promotional Mix**

6. **Customer Relations**

7. **Image Review**

The internet is an excellent source for gathering market research data. In addition to the U.S. government web-site, the following web-sites will be helpful:

> Better business Bureau – www.bbb.org
> Census Bureau – www.census.gov
> General Printing Office – www.gpo.gov
> Federal Trade Commission – www.ftc.gov
> U. S. Department of commerce – www.doc.gov
> SEC's Edgar Database – www.sec.gov/edgarhp.htm
> Free EDGAR – www.freeedgar.com
> Edgar Online – www.edgar-online.com
> Robert Morris & Associates – www.rma.org

FINAL THOUGHTS

"All that we do is done with an eye to something else."
Aristotle

Communication is civilization. Since the beginning of time, thoughts, ideas, intentions, desires were conveyed either by gestures, oral, written, numerical, and music. It has allowed advancement of culture and commerce and continues to do so today.

Communication, nothing will happen without it. As a business owner, entrepreneur, manager and leader of people, you soon realize that to maximize your efforts and goals the cooperation and assistance of others is necessary. The ability to be persuasive in communicate your desires, information, and mission in a convincing, understandable, motivating way will great assist in achieving the desired end. The art of conveying parallel interest in your endeavor will inspire others to join and participate with you. As such you must know and anticipate your audience to speak to them in their language of appreciation to clearly communicate in a concise, succinct, manner. This includes the financial language of business for it is what speaks to financial types like investors, creditors, and vendors. Upon being presented with the all-important Business Plan, these will first read the financials and if feasible will then go on to the other parts of interest. If not, they will go no further and your opportunity to communicate the business model, the way you will make money, will go no further. Whether you are a start-up venture seeking initial capital, a thriving business wanting additional working capital or long-term money to expand, your ability to communicate the mutual advantages of such an investment is the life-blood of your vision.

Therefore, in addition to all the tools of effective speaking and writing, learn to speak the language of lenders and investors to present your business model in the most favorable way that appeals to them, the parallel interest.

Communication is dynamic. Communication is essential. Communication is vital.

ABOUT THE AUTHOR

Daniel R. Hogan, Jr., Ph.D. MBA
Louisiana Civil Law Notary

Dr. Hogan is a career banker, financier, and educator; He organized and obtained approval for a national bank and a state bank. Prior to being Chairman of the Board and President of these banks, he was Senior Vice President and Chairman of the Commercial Loan Committee of the former National Bank of Commerce, a multi-billion-dollar bank. Concurrently with organizing the new banks, in 1985 he incorporated, and presently operates as President, Hogan Financial Corporation, *"The Entrepreneur's Edge"*, a commercial lending and consulting company, and as of January 2003 organized and incorporated Hogan Business School, Inc., *"The Entrepreneur's Source"*.

He is at present or formerly a Visiting Professor at, Nunez Community College, University of Holy Cross, Delgado Community College, Loyola University, Concordia College, and the University of New Orleans with emphasis on Economics, Finance, Entrepreneurship, Franchising, and Management Skills. He has served as a business consultant at the University of New Orleans Small Business Development Center and has conducted various SBDC entrepreneur, business and banking seminars. He is an instructor for the Kauffman Foundation's FastTrac Entrepreneur Learning Program. He has taught at the American Institute of Banking. He served as a member of the Board of Directors of the University of New Orleans International Alumni Association and a member of the Managing Committee, Chairman of the Strategic Management Committee.

He holds a Doctor of Philosophy in Business Administration from Kennedy-Western University-Dissertation *"Effect of Entrepreneur Leadership on Management"*, Master of Business Administration and Bachelor of Science Business Administration Degrees from the University of New Orleans, a Graduate Commercial Lending Certificate from the University of Oklahoma and a Graduate Commercial Banking Certificate from the

Louisiana State University Graduate School of Banking. He has earned a certificate designation as a CFE, Certified Franchise Executive, from the University of Texas at El Paso, and is a Dun & Bradstreet Certified Financial and Credit Analyst.

Having sat for and passed the State of Louisiana Examination requirements; he has been sworn in as a Louisiana Civil Law Notary and is empowered as a Notary Public in the State of Louisiana, Orleans Parish.

Personal Motto: *"It's Always Too Soon To Give Up!"*

APPENDIX

A-1

BUSINESS PLAN OUTLINE

Table of Contents

COVER LETTER

EXECUTIVE SUMMARY

THE COMPANY

THE PRODUCT

MARKETING

MANAGEMENT

FACILITY

FINANCIAL

COVER LETTER

The following is an example of how a letter of introduction to a lender or investor could read.

Dear Lender:

My name is _____ and I am in the _____ business. The business has been (will be) operating (opening) _____. The location is easily accessible, and the population base is appropriate for _____ (type of business).

I have determined the total asset needs of the business to be $ _____. I will contribute _____% of the needed capital ($_____). We are seeking debt financing in the amount of $ _____. The loan will be repaid in monthly installments of $ _____ over a period of _____ years. The proceeds of the loan will be distributed as follows: $ _____ for land, $ _____ for building improvements, $ _____ equipment, $ _____ for inventory, and the remaining $ _____ will be held as working capital.

A current balance sheet, list of collateral, 12-month pro-forma income statement, 12-month pro-forma cash flow, two-year pro-forma income statement, and break-even analysis are included in the attached business plan under the finance section. Your prompt consideration is appreciated. If additional information is needed, please contact:

Your Name
Your Address
Your City, State and Zip Code
Phone Number Including Area Code
E-mail address

Sincerely,

Your Name

EXECUTIVE SUMMARY

The executive summary is the last thing written and one of the first things read. It should be clear, concise, accurate and inviting. The goal of the executive summary is to summarize each major section of the business plan. Try to limit your summary to one or two paragraphs per section. Do not introduce anything in this section that is not supported in the body of the plan. Remember, a summary just focuses on the main points that your intended reader wants or needs to know.

- **Company Summary**

Focus on ownership, structure, history, and size. Include a brief overview of the history of your business, plus a summary of current activities

- **Product or Service Summary**

Focus on your products, what makes them better or different, pricing, gross profit margin of goods, and any patents or other protection you have.

- **Market Summary**

Focus on your geographic market area, customer profile or target market, market opportunities, industry trends, and sales potential. Make sure you demonstrate that you understand your market and industry.

- **Management Summary**

Focus on the management expertise, who will be making the decisions and who will be running the business daily. Show that you have the right people doing the right things. You will need resumes as well as a summary of experience, qualifications and credentials for all owners and key members of your management team.

- **Financial Summary**

Focus on owners' equity injection, time and sales volume necessary to break-even, your financial needs and your ability to service the debt. You want to summarize how the proposed loan will be used, and how it will be repaid and how it will benefit your business. Include projected income and cash-flow statements for two to three years. Your assumptions should be clearly stated and realistic. The loan package must include both business and personal financial statements. Make sure that you fully understand the "story" that your financial statements tell.

THE COMPANY

This is a profile of the company and is usually one or two pages. In a start-up company this should illustrate how you envision the company. In an existing company you should explain the "before" and "after" position of the company.

- When was the company founded; by whom?

    Give company history and if a start-up, explain how and when you plan to be operational. If it is an existing business, what events happened to need a bank loan or expansion, etc.?

- Ownership Structure - Is it a sole proprietor, corporation, partnership? Who are the owners and what is their ownership position? If the business is a partnership, then include a partnership agreement in the appendix.
- Mission Statement - Why are you in business? What are you trying to accomplish?
- What type of business?

    Retail

    Manufacturing

    Service

- What type of products?
- What target markets do you intend to serve?
- How large is the company? You can use the number of employees, average monthly payroll, and sales number of units per month, etc. to illustrate the size of the company.

    When the reader leaves this section, he should know the company's history, ownership, product offering, target market, and size of company.

THE PRODUCT

This section is designed to educate the reader about your product or service. Discuss in detail your product's specifications, patents, unique characteristics, costs, sales price, and other similar information. Organize this section according to similar product and service categories and discuss each category separately. It is not uncommon to have several categories or departments. For example, a convenience store might have the following categories: gasoline, drinks, canned goods, alcoholic beverages, diary, and snacks. You should address the following issues for each product/service category or department.

- Detailed description of products or services
  Are your products name brand products, or a mix of name brand products and generic products? How many different types of products, colors, styles, and models do you carry? If you manufacture your product, include a drawing or sketch as an exhibit. How is the product used? Is it used in conjunction with other products?
- Patents, Copyrights, and Trade secrets
- Your product's competitive edge or strengths

  What makes your product or service different? Are you the only distributor? Why would anyone use your product over another product?

- R & D efforts and future products

  Are you going to have other products on the "drawing board"? If so, discuss them.

- Product sales

  What percent do you expect each category of products and services to contribute to total sales?

- Product margins

  Describe the price-vs.-cost relationship. This information will help develop part of the pro-forma income statement. You can use the gross margin approach (price - variable costs = gross margin), or the mark-up approach (cost divided by sales price = markup).

- Inventory

Does this product/service require an inventory? If so, how much inventory for each category of goods and how much will it cost? How many times in a year does it turn over? Is it perishable? What is the product's shelf-life?

- Suppliers

Who are your suppliers and what is the lead time on orders? If one supplier goes out of business are there other sources of suppliers?

When the reader leaves this section, they should know how you will make your revenue, how much gross profit margin each category of products or services will make, what percent of total sales each product will account for, and the products competitive strengths.

MARKETING

This section should present the facts to convince the investor or banker that your product or service has a market in a growing industry and can win sales from the competition. This is one of the more difficult sections to prepare. This section represents the most risk to a business. The Marketing Plan helps to reduce that risk, spot problems and potential problems in your current market, identify sales opportunities and get basic facts about your market to help make better decisions and set up plans of action. It is best to complete this section of the business plan early since all estimates of future sales come from the market analysis. Contrary to popular belief, a business does not sell to "everyone." Therefore, it is important to accurately identify your customer base.

This section should address:

1. Market Size
   - Describe the total geographic market area that you intend to serve.
   - What does this total market look like in terms of demographic variables like age, sex, income, etc.?
   - Estimate the total market size by each market segment.
2. Industry
   - What are sales for the industry as a whole?
   - Identify any recent trends in the industry. Is demand for this product or service increasing, decreasing; If so, why?
   - Are the sales seasonal? If so, what are the busy months?
3. Customer Analysis
   - Describe your specific customers using a demographic profile. For example, age, sex, income, etc.
   - Identify where your customers are located (city, zip code, neighborhood, etc.)
   - How many people fit your customer profile in the area you want to target? You can find this in demographic books at the library.
   - Explain why your customers come to you instead of the competition (competitive advantage).
4. Potential Market

- Show how you calculated your potential market. Include things like how often they will purchase, which products/services they will purchase, and average amount of each purchase. Be sure to consider the seasonality of sales. Some products are sold only at one time of the year (Christmas) and others are sold year-round (gasoline).

Strengths and Weaknesses of the Competition

- Identify and discuss each major competitor and their market share.
- Do a S.W.O.T. analysis. That is, assess the competition's Strengths, Weaknesses, Opportunities and Threats. Knowing the competition's strengths and weaknesses can help you develop a strategy that takes advantage of their weaknesses while avoiding their strengths. Your ability to take advantage of an opportunity in the market may threaten the competition and keep them off balance.
- You need to indicate who are the industry leaders in service, pricing, performance, cost and quality; discuss any firms that have recently entered or dropped out of the industry.

5. Advertising Plan

- Are you going to find your customers or are they going to find you?
- How are you going to advertise to them - Radio, TV, mail, fliers, signs, yellow pages, etc.? For example, advertising eye glasses on a youth-oriented rock-n-roll radio station may not work well, but it might work on a more adult oriented radio talk show.
- When will you advertise and how often?
- How much will it cost to advertise? What percentage of sales will it represent?

6. Marketing Plan

- In retail business, how will you cultivate more sales? Will you use direct sales, direct mail, coupons, and promotions with other vendors?
- In a service company, how will you generate sales leads? Will you use seminars, trade shows, telephone sales, purchase client lists or customized mailing lists?

The reader should leave this section with a clear understanding of your geographic market, target markets, potential of each of those markets, your share of the potential market, and how you are going to communicate with those markets.

MANAGEMENT & LABOR

This section should identify owners with 20% or more ownership who could influence the business. This section should illustrate that the right people are in charge and doing the right things. The management should have experience in the industry or at the very least similar experience in a similar industry. If you do not possess the right skills then you may need to hire an employee or a consultant with those skills.

This section should address the following:

- Ownership and owner's compensation

Who owns what percent of the company? What are the owners' responsibilities and how much are they being paid?

- Other investors

Who are they and how are they going to be paid back for their investment?

- Key management and experience

Give names, resumes and brief backgrounds on all key people. These people should know what they are doing and have experience doing it. What are their job responsibilities and how much will they be paid?

- Employees

Identify your labor needs. List the type and number of employees. Will they need any training, licenses or certifications? What are their duties, estimated total labor hours, and how much you will pay them?

- Professional Advisors
  Accountants
  Attorneys
  Consultants

The reader should leave this section with some degree of confidence that the people in charge have assembled a team that will run the business profitably.

FACILITY

This section should discuss all issues pertaining to the facility.

- Location

Is the location appropriate for this type of business? Are there any complimentary businesses nearby? If so, discuss them.

- Zoning

Is the location zoned for this type of commerce?

- Utilities

Is there adequate power for your needs? If not, how much will it cost to up-grade it?

- What are the store hours?
- Lease or purchase

Will you purchase the building? If so, how much will it cost? If you will lease, for how long and how much is the lease? Will you have to do any construction or improvements to make it ready for business?

- Parking

Is there adequate parking for your customers?

- Inventory

How much space do you need, and can you accommodate it?

- Monthly fixed costs

What will be the fixed costs that you expect to incur on a monthly basis? Include things like rent, utilities, telephone, insurance maintenance, salaries, etc.

- Overhead

How much will it cost to operate the facility per department, per hour, per product? That is, how much should each department or product is charged for its share of the overhead? (Fixed monthly costs)?

The reader should leave this section with a clear understanding of the costs associated with running the facility

FINANCIAL

The financial section consists of several pro-forma financial statements that are generated from the previous sections. In some ways, the other sections of the business plan are just supporting information for the financial section. To build the financial statements the previous sections of the business plan are combined with the following information.

- List of startup costs
- Capital equipment expenditures
- Depreciation schedule
- List of collateral
- Sources and uses of financing – a detailed statement of how you will use the loan proceeds. Don't forget to include the proceeds of the loan in your cash-flow projections (and the interest expense in your projected income statement).

    Amount – Remember that you are offering the bank/investor a deal that will make them money; you are not asking for an allowance. The attitude you should have is to ask, "This is how much money I need, and how much will they lend/invest?" and not, "Will they lend/invest it?"

    Repayment Plan – You will have to make some assumptions about the terms of the loan or the investment in your proposal.

The following are the typical financial statements found in a business plan financial section.

- Balance Sheet after start-up, loan, or expansion
- 12-month projected cash flow statements on a month-by-month basis
- 12-month projected income statements on a month-by-month basis
- annual projected balance sheets and income statement for two to three years
- Break-even analysis
- Ratio analysis
- Assumptions used in financial statements

BREAKEVEN ANALYSIS

Sales Price per Unit Less Variable Costs per Unit =

Contribution Margin $ _____

OR

Total Sales Less Total Variable Cost =

Total Contribution Margin $_____

Contribution Margin Divided by Sales Price =

Contribution Ratio   _____%

OR

Total Contribution Margin Divided by Total Sales =

Contribution Ratio   _____%

Total Fixed Costs $ _____

Breakeven in Number of Units =

Total Fixed Costs divided by

Total Contribution Margin   Units _____

Breakeven in Sales =

Total Fixed Costs divided by

Contribution Ratio   Sales _____

APPENDIX

The appendix is where you put supporting data that does not easily fit into the business plan narrative.

- Market research data
- Resumes of key owners and managers
- Personal financial statements of owners with 20% or more ownership
- Patent or product information
- Leases
- Contracts
- Articles of incorporation or partnership agreement
- Newspaper or magazine articles relating to the product or industry
- Other supporting data

A-1A

THE BUSINESS PLAN PRESENTATION

Purpose:

- To persuade stakeholders to cooperate, support, participate in the venture

Four Steps:

- Establish credibility
- Frame goals of venture to be consistent with goals of investors establish common ground with the listener
- Offer solid compelling evidence to support the plan
- Build a good relationship with potential investors demonstrate your passion and commitment to the plan

Four-Part Pitch:

- Problem that customers need to solve
- Customers with this problem have money to spend in resolving it
- This plan, this company, has a profitable and proven solution to the problem
- The management of this plan, this company, has implemented effectively in the past, and can execute well, again, in the future

Nine questions to answer in the Business Plan Presentation:

- What is the product/service and what problem is being it solved?
- What are its unique benefits?
- How will it be distributed and sold
- How much will it cost to deliver
- Who is the customer
- How many people will buy it the first and second year
- What is the sales price?
- When will you break even
- Who are the key team members and how are they qualified to build this business?

Ten slide presentations: Seldom more than ten and no more than 30 words per slide. Presentation should not be longer than 20 minutes.

- Company name, presenters' names, contact information
- Description of the product, the need and the market
- Solution: the product and its key benefits
- Business model and profitability
- Competition and strategy
- Technology and related processes (if any)
- Marketing and sales plans
- Leadership team and prior experience
- Financial projections summary
- Current status and funds required

A-2

77 QUESTIONS EVERY BUSINESS PLAN SHOULD ANSWER

1. Why will this business succeed?
2. Why is this product or service useful?
3. What will the product do for the user?
4. What is the expected life cycle of the product?
5. How do advances in technology affect your product and business?
6. What is the product liability?
7. What makes this business and product unique?
8. Does the product meet a specific need or perceived need of the customer?
9. Does the product have brand-name recognition?
10. Are there repeat uses for the product?
11. Is this a high quality or low-quality product?
12. Is the consumer the end user of the product?
13. Are there any substitutes for your product?

14. Do you lease or own the property/facilities?
15. What are the terms of your lease?
16. How much do you owe on the mortgage?
17. Are the facilities adequate for future expansion based on your business plan?
18. Will the expansion require relocation?
19. Who owns the patent?
20. What licensing arrangements have been made between you and the patent company?
21. Does anyone else have a licensing arrangement? If so, how does this impact your company?
22. Why does this business have high growth potential?
23. What makes this business situation special?
24. Does this product have mass appeal or single large buyers?
25. How large is the customer base?
26. What is the typical demographic of your customer base?
27. What are the current market trends?
28. What are the seasonal effects in your industry?
29. What advantages does your competition have over you?
30. What advantages do you have over your competition?
31. Compared to your competition, how do you compete in terms of price, performance, service and warranties?
32. What is the lag time between initial buyer contact and the actual sale?
33. How does your company and product fit into the industry?
34. What are the keys to success in your industry?

35. How did you determine total sales of the industry and its growth rate?
36. What industry changes most affect your company's profits?
37. Who is your competition?
38. Do your competitors have an advantage due to equipment?
39. What makes your business different?
40. Why will your business succeed when it must compete with larger companies?
41. How do you expect the competition to react to your company?
42. If you plan to take market share, how will you do it?
43. What are the critical elements of your marketing plan?
44. Is this primarily a retail or industrial marketing strategy?
45. How important is advertising in your marketing plan?
46. How sensitive are sales to your advertising plan?
47. How will your marketing strategy change as the product/or industry matures?
48. Is direct selling necessary?
49. What is the capacity of your facility?
50. Where do you see bottlenecks developing?
51. How important is quality control?
52. What is the current backlog?
53. Is the product assembly line based or individually customized?
54. What are the health and safety concerns in producing this product?
55. Who are your suppliers and how long have they been in business?

56. How many sources of suppliers are there?
57. Currently, are there any shortages in components?
58. How old is your company's equipment?
59. What is the yearly maintenance cost?
60. What is the current research and development?
61. What is the annual expenditure on R&D?
62. How does R&D impact future sales?
63. What type of business experience does the management team have?
64. Are the members achievers?
65. What motivates each team member?
66. Can the team accomplish the job outlined in the business plan?
67. How many employees do you have?
68. What is the anticipated need in the immediate future?
69. Where does the labor supply come from?
70. What is the employee break down, i.e. full time, part time, managerial staff, support staff, production/service?
71. What is the cost of training?
72. Is the labor force primarily skilled or unskilled workers?
73. Is there a union and what is the company's relationship?
74. What are your capital requirements over the next five years?

75. For what will the capital raised via the plan be used?

76. What is the exit strategy? (How will investors get their money out?)

77. What return on investment can the investors expect?

A-3

MISSION STATEMENTS

Five keys to designing a Mission Statement

1. ***Keep it short.*** It must be understandable and memorable for all who encounter it. While principally written to guide employees, the statement also speaks to customers, vendors, stockholders, and creditors.

2. ***Keep it simple.*** It has to a statement that everyone can learn and understand. A mission statement that is not shared or poorly communicated has little value to the company.

3. ***Keep it straightforward.*** It must be able to guide everyone in the company every day. It must be actionable, something that helps the employees make active decisions without having to refer everything to a superior. It should guide everyone in the company to the goals that the owner has set; it helps to ensure that all are headed in the same direction.

4. ***Keep it clear.*** It must tell everyone exactly what you do and conversely it will tell them what you do not do.

5. ***Keep it measurable.*** There should be a benchmark for every part of the statement to determine if the goals of the statement are being met.

SAMPLES:

American Red Cross – The American Red Cross is a humanitarian service organization, led by volunteers, that provides relief to victims of disasters and helps people prevent, prepare for and respond to emergencies.

Apex Elevator – To provide a high reliability, error-free method for moving people and products up, down, and sideways within a building.

Josephson Drug Company, Inc. – To provide people with longer lives and higher-quality lives by applying research efforts to develop new or improved drugs and health-care products.

McDonald's – To satisfy the world's appetite for good food, well-served, at a price people can afford.

Chrysler Corporation – Chrysler Corporation is committed to providing our customers with the world's highest level of satisfaction with our products and service.

Hogan Financial Corporation – Organized to assist entrepreneurs with the skills, knowledge, and financial resources to start, grow, and manage a profitable business; and to assist individuals with the realization of financial dreams and aspirations.

A–4

VISUAL AID USAGE

1. Keep the exhibit out of sight until you are ready to use it.
2. Use exhibits and power points large enough to be seen from the last row.
3. Never pass an exhibit around while you are speaking.
4. When showing an exhibit or power point, make sure all can see it.
5. A moving exhibit is worth more than one that does not unless it distracts from the message.
6. Don't stare at the exhibit as you talk – you are trying to communicate with the audience not the exhibit.
7. When you are finish with the exhibit, get it out of sight if practicable.

Visual materials and power points are becoming more prominent as devices to promote clarity. There is no better way to ensure that your audience will understand what you have to say than to go before them prepared to show as well as to tell them what you have in mind. If a visual aid does not explain better than words than it should not be used.

They show how things look; how they work; and how things relate to each other. Use the simplest terms and shortest words possible avoiding complete sentences. Show only the highlights will more elaboration coming from you. Use a minimum number of graphs and don't use vertical printing that the audience must tilt their head to view.

OPTIONS:

- Overhead transparencies
- Electronic presentations, PowerPoint slide show
- Chalkboards and whiteboards
- Flip charts
- Other visuals, samples, models.

A–5

TEN THINGS THAT WILL GET YOU FIRED

1. **Don't bother learning what's expected of you:** Make sure you understand exactly what your job entails, your deadlines and any relevant policies. This eliminates ambiguity and ensures you'll know how your performance measures up.

2. **Learn to say, "That's not part of my job description."** Everyone needs to set limits but doing only the bare minimum sends a clear message that you're just interested in a regular paycheck. Sooner or later your boss will start looking for someone willing to take more initiative.

3. **Go shopping in the supply closet:** while you at it run a few errands with the company car and pad your expense report. Stealing from the company is one of the best ways to guarantee your immediate dismissal.

4. **Abuse company technology:** Think your boss won't mine that you spend more time instant messaging your friends than you do working? Think again. Most companies monitor all their employee's emails and internet usage. Never use your company computer for anything illegal or X-rated.

5. **Complain about your job to anyone who will listen:** Whether your pay is too low, the work is drudgery, or you think your boss ia an idiot, be careful of who hears you

complain. If it gets back to your boss, he/she may just put you out of your misery.

6. **Forget teamwork-look out for number one:** No one wants to work with an arrogant employee who steals ideas or an egotistical worker who demeans others. Helping your co-workers doesn't make you a pushover, it makes you smart. Likable employees move up the company ranks more quickly, and your colleagues will be more likely to help you find leads when you launch your next job search.

7. **Bring your personal life to work:** It is inevitable that personal business is going to pop up during work hours. Keep personal call and errands to a minimum during work hours.

8. **Consistently work abbreviated workdays:** Want to show your boss how little you care about your job? Regularly come in late and leave early. If you can't be trusted to show up on time, how can you be trusted with more responsibility?

9. **Treat deadlines more like guidelines:** When you procrastinate, everyone suffers. Your missed deadline reflects poorly on you, your co-workers, and your boss.

10. **Operate the gossip mill:** While you can't avoid office gossip completely, don't get caught spreading it. Do you really want hurtful or untrue rumors to be traced back to you?

A–6

THE PROBLEM WITH RULES

Rules are external

They are made by others

They present us with a puzzle to be solved and loopholes to be found.

We are ambivalent about rules

We know we need some and we want others to play by them,

But we say, "Rules are meant to be broken."

Rules are reactive

They respond to past events

Rules are both over and under inclusive

Because they are proxies, they cannot be precise.

Proliferation of rules is a tax on the system

Few people can remember them all.

We lose productivity when we stop to look them up.

Rules are typically prohibitions

They speak to *can* and *can't*.

We view them as confining and constricting.

Rules require enforcement

With laxity, they lose credibility and effectiveness.

They necessitate expensive bureaucracies of compliance.

Rules speak to boundaries and floors

But create inadvertent ceilings

We can't legislate "The sky's the limit."

The only way to honor rules is to obey them exactly

They speak to coercion and motivation.

The inspiration to excel must come from somewhere else.

Too many rules breed overreliance

We think, "If it mattered, they would have made a rule."

A-7

COMMUNICATION INTERVIEW

Ask the following questions of your employer, manager or another business owner/manager.

A. How important is communication to the successful performance of your job/success of your business?

B. How do you communicate with your employees, customers, and superiors?

C. What is an example of a successful communication experience you have had?

D. What is an example of an unsuccessful communication experience you have had?

E. What communication barriers do you commonly encounter?

F. What does organizational goodwill and company culture mean to you?

G. What recommendations do you have for someone who wants to improve his or her communication skills?

H. What was your hardest communication lesson or biggest communication mistake?

A-8

THE ENTREPRENEURIAL PROCESS TO START, GROW, AND MANAGE A BUSINESS

- **Decision to become an Entrepreneur**
  To be their own boss
  To pursue their own ideas
  To realize financial rewards

- **Developing Successful Business Ideas**
  Opportunity recognition and generation of ideas
  Feasibility analysis
  Industry and competitor analysis
  Developing an effective business model

- **Moving from an Idea to an Entrepreneurial Firm**
  Building a new venture team
  Assessing a new venture's financial strength and viability
  Preparing a proper ethical and legal foundation, and appropriate form of Business ownership
  Writing a Business Plan
  Getting financing or funding

- **Managing and Growing an Entrepreneurial Firm**
  Marketing Issues, the 5 "P's"-
  (Product, Price, Promotion. Place, People)
  Importance of Intellectual Property

Preparing for and evaluating the Challenges of Growth
Strategies for Growth – Franchising

The four main characteristics of successful entrepreneur managers are:

1. Passion for the Business
2. Customer and Product focus
3. Tenacity and Persistence despite failure
4. Execution Intelligence
5.

Eight Tips for Entrepreneurs

1. Work for Self
2. Get Organized and Communicate
3. Take risk
4. Innovate
5. Seize Opportunity
6. Overcome Adversity and don't take No for an Answer
7. Sell; ABC (Always Be Closing)
8. Business Can Be War

GLOSSARY

A

Accounting – process of collecting, recording, reporting, and analyzing a firm's financial activities

Agent - person who agrees to act for the benefit of another

Amortization – the gradual reduction of debts by periodic payments

Antitrust law - legislation intended to prohibit attempts to monopolize markets

Arbitrage - buying at a low price in one market and selling at a higher price in another

Assets – items owned by an entity

B

Balance sheet – financial statement that shows what a business owns and owes at a specific moment in time, a snap-shot of financial status

Bankruptcy – situation when a business cannot meet financial obligations and liabilities exceed assets, and the firm seeks legal protection to repay or restructure debts

Barriers to entry – conditions that create disincentives to enter an industry

Barter – the direct exchange of goods rather than for cash

Board of Directors – group of stockholders elected individuals who oversee governance of an organization

Break-even point – the sales level where revenues equal cost

Budget deficit – government expenditures are greater than tax revenues

Budget surplus – tax revenues are greater than government expenditures

Business – an enterprise that is started and operated for the purpose of its owners

Business ethics – application of moral standards and values to business situations

Business model – a plan that indicates how the aspects of the business work together to generate a profit – how the business makes money

Business plan – written document describing all aspects of the business to determine feasibility, raise money, and provide a plan of operation

Burn rate – rate in which a business is spending its money until it reached profits

C

Capital – produced goods that are used in the production of other goods, wealth in any form that can be used to produce more wealth, the ownership equity in a business

Capital investment – money used to purchase permanent fixed assets for a business

Cash basis accounting – accounting method that recognizes revenues and expenses when cash is received or paid out

Cash flow – cash generated after expenses, taxes, and adding back non-cash expenses

Cash management – process of forecasting, collecting, disbursing, investing, and planning for the cash a business needs to operate smoothly

Checkable deposits – deposits in banks or other financial institutions on which checks can be written

Code of ethics – written document that describes the company's general value system, moral principles, and specific ethical rules

Collective bargaining – union bargains with management on behalf of the workers

Common stock – security with voting power representing an ownership right in a corporation

Comparative advantage – when one nation or company can produce a good at a lower opportunity cost than another

Compound interest – interest paid on interest

Conflict of Interest – situation in which one relationship or obligations places you in direct conflict with an existing relationship or obligation

Contraction – the phase of the business cycle when real GDP is decreasing

Contraction fiscal policy – a decrease in government expenditures or an increase in taxation

Contraction monetary policy – a decrease in the money supply

Copyright – government granted monopoly on the production and sale of a creative work granted to the creator

Corporation – an organization owned by stockholders that is considered a separate legal entity apart from its owners

Crowding out – occurs when increases in government spending lead to decreases in private spending

Culture – a set of attitudes, beliefs, and practices that characterize a group of individuals

Currency – coins and paper money issued by the federal government

Current assets – assets that can or will be converted to cash within the next 12 months

Current liabilities – obligations that are due within the next 12 months

Current ratio – the ratio of current assets to current liabilities indicating liquidity

D

Debt ratio – the ratio of total liabilities to total assets measuring the percentage of assets financed by debt

Debt-to-equity ratio – ratio of total liabilities to equity indicating how leverage the business is

Deflation – a decrease in the price level

Demand – the willingness and ability of buyers to buy different quantities of goods at different prices

Developed country – has a relatively high per capital real Gross Domestic Product (GDP)

Depreciation – non-cash expense allocating an asset's original cost over the time it is expected to produce revenue

Discount rate – interest rate the Fed charges banks for borrowed reserves

Disposable income – household income after taxes

Dividend – portion of after-tax profits distributed to shareholders

Dumping – the practice of selling exports at a price below that charged in the home country

E

Economic growth – increase in the productive capacity of an economy

Economic system – the way in which a society answers economic questions

Economics – study of how societies use their limited resources to try to satisfy their unlimited wants

Economies of scale – exist when as production is increased and average cost decreases

Elasticity – a measure of the responsiveness of one variable to changes in another variable

Employed – those with paying jobs

Entrepreneurship – the special skills involved in organizing the factors of production, labor, land, and capital, for profit

Equilibrium price – price where quantity demanded equals quantity supplied

Equity – the book value of a business after all debts and other claims, the amount of cash the business owners have invested in the business plus any retained earnings.

Ethics – a set of moral standards and values that help choose between right and wrong

Ethical Dilemma – situation in which there is no obvious right or wrong decision, but rather a right or right answer

Expansion – phase of the business cycle when real GDP is increasing

Expansion fiscal policy – increase in government expenditures or a decrease in taxation

Expansion monetary policy – increase in the money supply

Exports – total foreign purchases of domestic goods

F

Federal funds rate – interest rate one bank charges another bank to borrow reserves (always below the Fed discount rate to avoid bank arbitrage)

Fiat money – money by government decree or fiat

Financial intermediation – process by which banks make depositors' savings available to borrowers

Financial statement – a report summarizing the financial condition of a business

Firm – an entity that employs resources to produce goods and services

Fiscal policy – changes in government expenditures and taxation to achieve economic goals

Fixed cost – cost that do not vary with output

Franchise – the rights to offer specific products or services under explicit guidelines at a certain location for a period

Free market – a market in which price is free to adjust up or down in response to demand and supply

G

GAAP – the generally accepted accounting principles that govern the accounting profession

Gross Domestic Product (GDP) – market of all final goods and services produced annually

Gross profit – amount earned after paying to produce or buy products but before deducting operating expense

Gross sales – total dollar amount of sales prior to expenses

Groupthink - a psychological phenomenon that occurs within a group of people in which the desire for harmony or conformity in the group results in an irrational or dysfunctional decision-making outcome. Group members try to minimize conflict and reach a consensus decision without critical evaluation of alternative viewpoints by actively suppressing dissenting viewpoints, and by isolating themselves from outside influences.

I

Imports – total domestic purchases of foreign goods

Incentive – changes the benefit or cost associated with an action

Income elasticity of demand – measures the responsiveness of demand to a change in income

Industry – a group of businesses producing similar products and services

Inflation – an increase in the price level

Internal locus of control – a belief that one's success depends on one's own efforts

Initial public offering (IPO) - the sale of shares of stock to the public for the first time

Interest – the payment for the use of loanable funds

Interest rate effect – when the price level decreases, the demand for money will decrease, causing interest rates to decrease

Intermediate good – a good that has not yet reached its final user, but is an input in the production of another good

Inverse relationship – as the value of one variable increases, the value of the other variable decreases

Investment – the acquisition of new physical capital

J

Joint venture – a business entered by two or more parties which is intended to terminate upon completion of a specific purpose

L

Labor – the physical and mental effort contributed to production

Labor force – the sum of the number of people employed plus the number unemployed

Laffer curve – indicates that lowering tax rates might increase tax revenues

Laissez-faire – policy that the government should not interfere with the economy

Land – naturally occurring resources

Law of demand – price and the quantity demanded of a good are inversely related

Law of diminishing marginal returns – as larger amount of a variable input are combined with fixed inputs, eventually the marginal physical product of the variable input declines

Legal barriers to entry – barriers to entry created by government action

Less developed country (LDC) – country with a relatively low per capital real GDP

License – a permit issued by the government authorizing a person to conduct a certain type of business

Limited liability company (LLC) – a hybrid organization offering the liability protection of a corporation but taxed as a partnership

Liquid asset – an asset that can be converted quickly into cash at a low transaction cost

Loopholes – exclusions and exemption from income, deductible expenses, and tax credits

M

M1 – currency in circulation plus checkable deposits

M2 – M1 plus small denomination time deposits, saving deposits, and money market accounts

M3 – everything in M2 plus some less liquid assets, large time deposits, term repurchase agreements, and term Eurodollars

Macroeconomics – branch of economics that focuses on overall economic behavior

Marginal cost – the change in total cost resulting from producing an additional unit of output

Marginal revenue – change in total revenue from selling one additional unit of output

Marginal utility – additional utility received from consuming an additional unit of a good

Market – all possible customers that might want a product or service at a price

Market mix – the combination of product, pricing, promotion, and place (distribution)

Merger – the combining of two separate companies into one

Microeconomics – the branch of economics that focuses on the components of the economy

Monetary base – currency in circulation plus bank reserves

Monetary policy – changes in the money supply to achieve macroeconomic goals

Money – whatever is generally accepted as a medium of exchange

Money creation – increases in checkable deposits made possible by fractional reserve banking

Monopolistic competition – many sellers of similar products

Monopoly – a firm that is a lone seller of a product with no close substitutes

N

National debt – the total amount the federal government owes its creditors

National defense argument – argument for certain trade restrictions based on national defense concerns

Natural monopoly – an industry in which economies of scale are so important only one firm can survive

Natural unemployment rate – the lowest unemployment rate that can be sustained without causing increasing inflation

Net exports – exports minus imports

Net worth – a firm's assets minus its liabilities

O

Oligopoly – an industry dominated by a few mutually interdependent firms

Open market operation – one of the tools of the Fed, buying and selling U.S. government securities in the open market

Opportunity cost – the value of the best alternative surrendered when a choice is made

Organization – an entity that involves people doing work for a purpose

P

Partnership – a firm owned and operated by two or more co-owners

Patent – a government granted monopoly on the production and sale of an invention

Peak – the highest phase of the business cycle

Per capital output – a basic measure of standard of living by dividing total output by the population

Perfect competition – many sellers of identical products

Poverty – a family whose income falls below a minimum established for an adequate standard of living

Preferred stock – stock that gives preference over common stock with respect to dividends or payment in the event of the company's sale or liquidation; may or may not have voting rights

Present value of an asset – the discounted value today of the income stream associated with the asset

Price ceiling – a maximum legal price

Price discrimination – occurs when a seller charges different prices to different buyers for the same good

Price floor – a minimum legal price

Prime rate – interest rate charged by banks to its preferential borrowers

Product differentiation – process of distinguishing a firm's product from similar products

Productivity – measured by the output produced per unit of input

Progressive tax – imposes higher tax rates on higher levels of income

Proportional tax – imposes the same tax rate on all levels of income

Proprietorship – a firm owned and operated by one individual

Prospectus – a complex document issued by a corporation in connection with the offering of securities containing specific information about the business, type of investment, financial data, and other pertinent facts in conformity with security regulations

Q

Quota – a legal limit on the quantity of a good that may be imported

R

Real GDP – GDP adjusted for changes in the price level

Real interest rate – the nominal interest rate minus the rate of inflation

Regressive tax – imposes higher tax rates on lower levels of income

Required reserves – the minimum amount of reserves that a bank is legally required to hold against it deposits

Reserves – vault cash plus bank deposits with the Federal Reserve

Resources – the inputs that makes production possible

Return on assets (ROA) – ratio of net profit to total assets

Return on equity (ROE) – ratio of net profit to equity

S

S corporation – a hybrid entity organized like a corporation but taxed like a partnership

Sarbanes-Oxley Act (SOX) – legislative response to the corporate accounting scandals

Say's law – supply creates its own demand

Scarcity – the problem that human wants exceed the production possible with the limited resources available

Self-sufficiency – a person uses their own resources to produce the goods and services that they want to consume

Shortage – when quantity demanded exceeds quantity supplied

Society – a structured community of people bound together by similar traditions, culture, and customs

Sunk cost – a past cost that cannot be changed by current decisions

Surplus – when quantity supplied exceeds quantity demanded

T

Tariff – a tax on an imported good

Trade deficit – when a nation's imports exceed its exports

Trade restrictions – government-imposed limitations on international trade

Transaction cost – the costs of bring buyers and sellers together for exchanges

Trough – the lowest phase of the business cycle

U

Unemployed – those without paying jobs who are actively seeking employment

Unemployment rate – the percentage of the labor force that is unemployed

Uniform commercial code (UCC) – set of business laws that provide a standard way to operate

U.S. government securities – debt instruments issued by the federal government

Utilitarianism – ethical choices that offer the greatest good for the greatest number of people

Utility – a measure of satisfaction received from consumption

V

Value – relative worth and importance

Value system – a set of personal principles formalized into a code of behavior

Variable cost – costs that vary with output

Velocity of money – the average number of times that a dollar is spent annually

Venture capital – early-stage private equity financing; these funds rank behind secured creditors

W

Whistle-Blower – an employee who discovers misconduct and chooses to bring it to the attention of others

Working capital – the excess of current assets over current liabilities

www.ingramcontent.com/pod-product-compliance
Lightning Source LLC
Chambersburg PA
CBHW030936180526
45163CB00002B/591